ALL ABOUT
SCIENCE

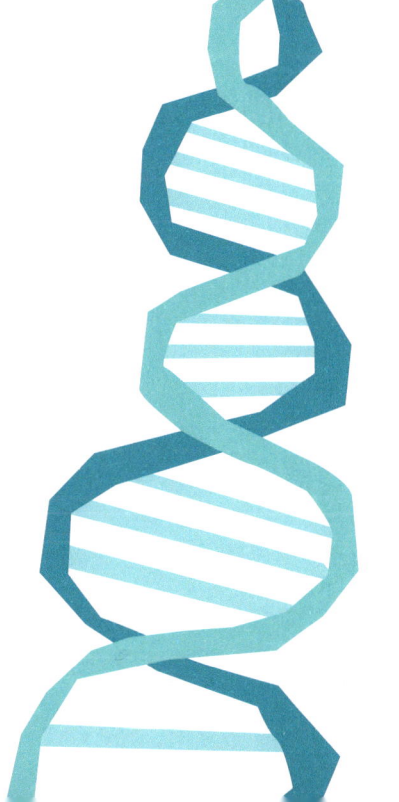

Published by Collins
An imprint of HarperCollins*Publishers*
1 Robroyston Gate
Glasgow
G33 1JN

HarperCollins*Publishers*
Macken House,
39/10 Mayor Street Upper,
Dublin 1, D01 C9W8, Ireland

collins.co.uk

First published 2025

© HarperCollins*Publishers* 2025

Collins® is a registered trademark of HarperCollins*Publishers* Ltd.

Text by: Sonya Newland
'Ask an expert' contribution by: Frida Akin-Taylor

Publisher: Beth Rogers
Project leader: Rachel Allegro
Cover and interior design: James Hunter & Rachel Allegro
Editorial: Tracey Cowell & Louise Robb
Production: Ilaria Rovera

Photo credits
All photos © Shutterstock, except: p.13(t): Contraband Collection / Alamy; p.13(b): PA Images / Alamy; p.14(br): IanDagnall Computing / Alamy; p.23(c): sciencephotos / Alamy; p.26: David Dugle / Alamy; p.47(t): Chris Hellier / Alamy; p.47(b): blickwinkel / Alamy; p.57(b): GRANGER - Historical Picture Archive / Alamy; p.69(b): IanDagnall Computing / Alamy; p.83(br): Sipa US / Alamy

All rights reserved. No part of this publication may be reproduced, stored in a retrieval system, or transmitted, in any form or by any means, electronic, mechanical, photocopying, recording or otherwise without the prior permission in writing of the publisher and copyright owners.

Without limiting the author's and publisher's exclusive rights, any unauthorised use of this publication to train generative artificial intelligence (AI) technologies is expressly prohibited. HarperCollins also exercise their rights under Article 4(3) of the Digital Single Market Directive 2019/790 and expressly reserve this publication from the text and data mining exception.

The contents of this publication are believed correct at the time of printing. Every care has been taken in the preparation of this book. However, the publisher can accept no responsiblity for errors or omissions, changes in detail given or for any expense or loss thereby caused.

A catalogue record for this book is available from the British Library.

ISBN 9780008737542

Printed by LEGO, Italy.

10 9 8 7 6 5 4 3 2 1

This book is produced from independently certified FSC™ paper to ensure responsible forest management. For more information visit: www.harpercollins.co.uk/green

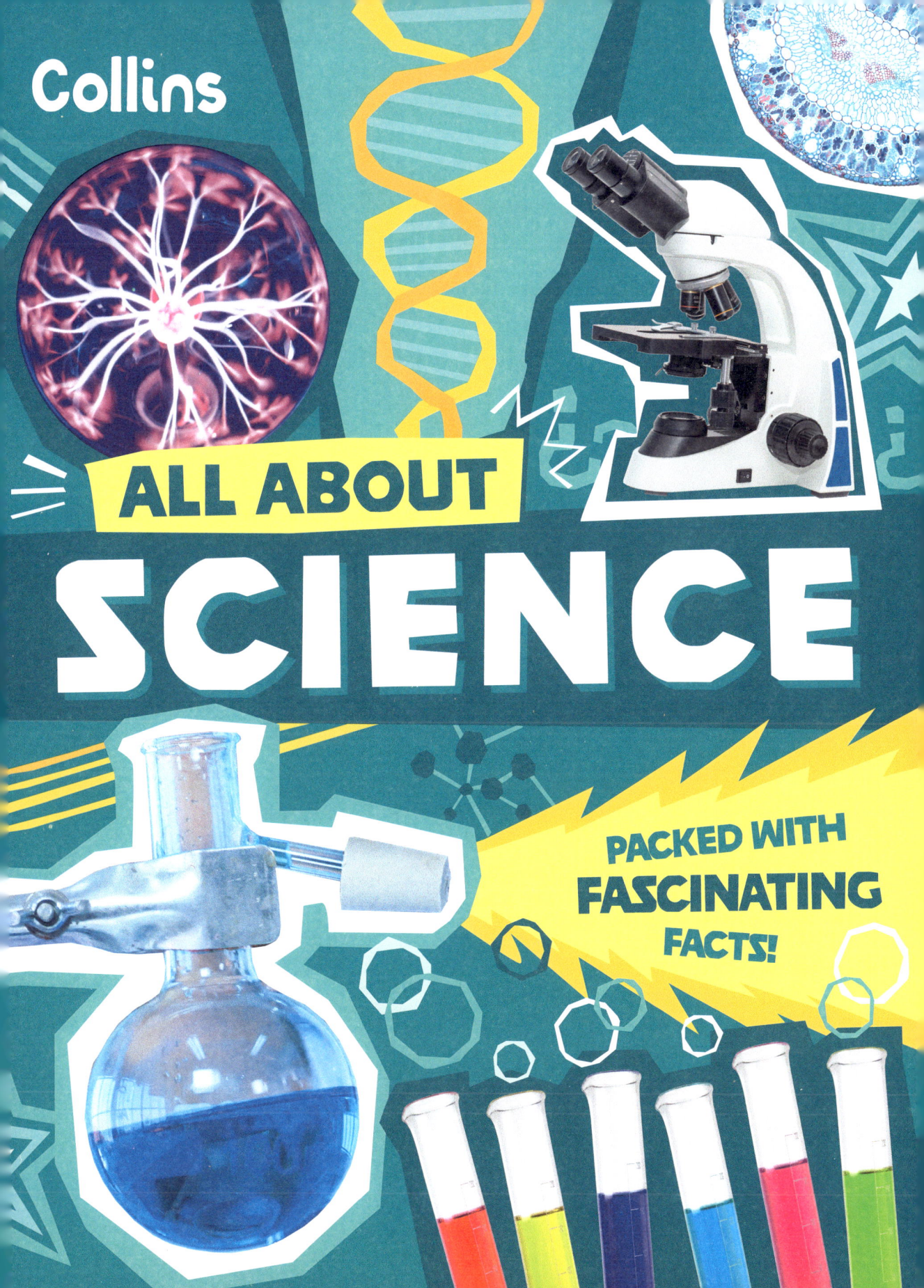

CONTENTS

What is science?	8
States of matter	10
Atoms	12
Molecules	14
The periodic table	16
Name that... Chemical element	18
Carbon	20
Metals	22
Super stats: Metals	24
Chemical reactions	26
Acids and alkalis	28
Materials	30
Name that... Material	32
The science of weather	34
Quiz yourself on... Chemistry	36
What is energy?	38
Energy sources	40
Light and colour	42
Reflection and refraction	44
Electricity	46
Magnets	48

Electromagnetism	50
What are forces?	52
Friction and resistance	54
Gravity	56
Speed and motion	58
Super stats: Fantastic forces	60
Quiz yourself on: Physics	62
The variety of life	64
Cells	66
DNA	68
Plants and photosynthesis	70
Quiz yourself on: Biology	72
Buildings and structures	74
Vehicles	76
Communication	78
Super stats: The internet	80
Inventions	82
Robotics	84
Ask an expert about: Engineering	86
Answers	88
Glossary	90
Index	94

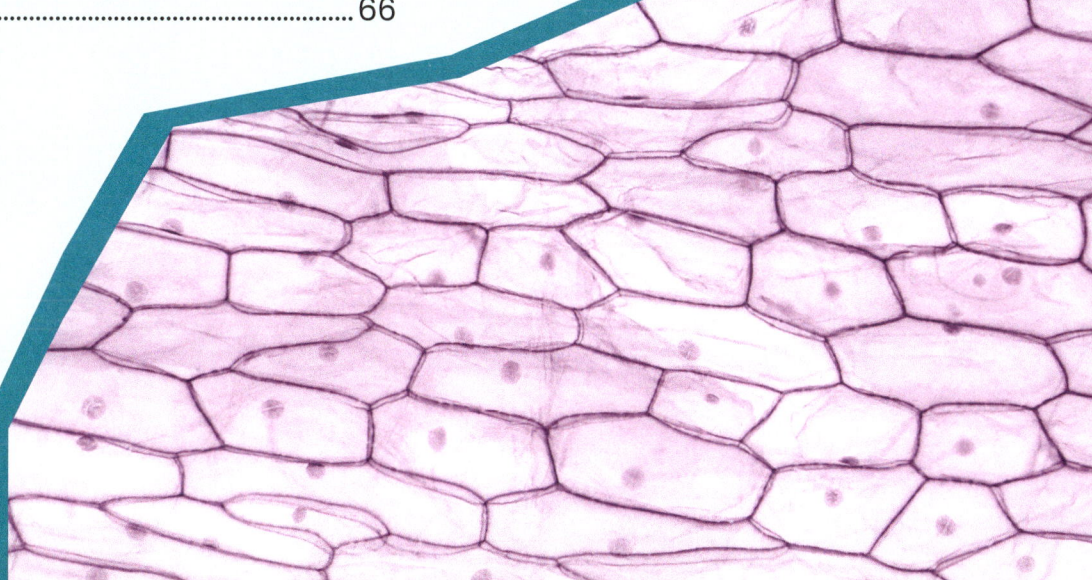

Super science

Science helps us make sense of the world around us – from studying the make-up of absolutely everything, to carrying out explosive experiments and engineering robots to perform complicated tasks.

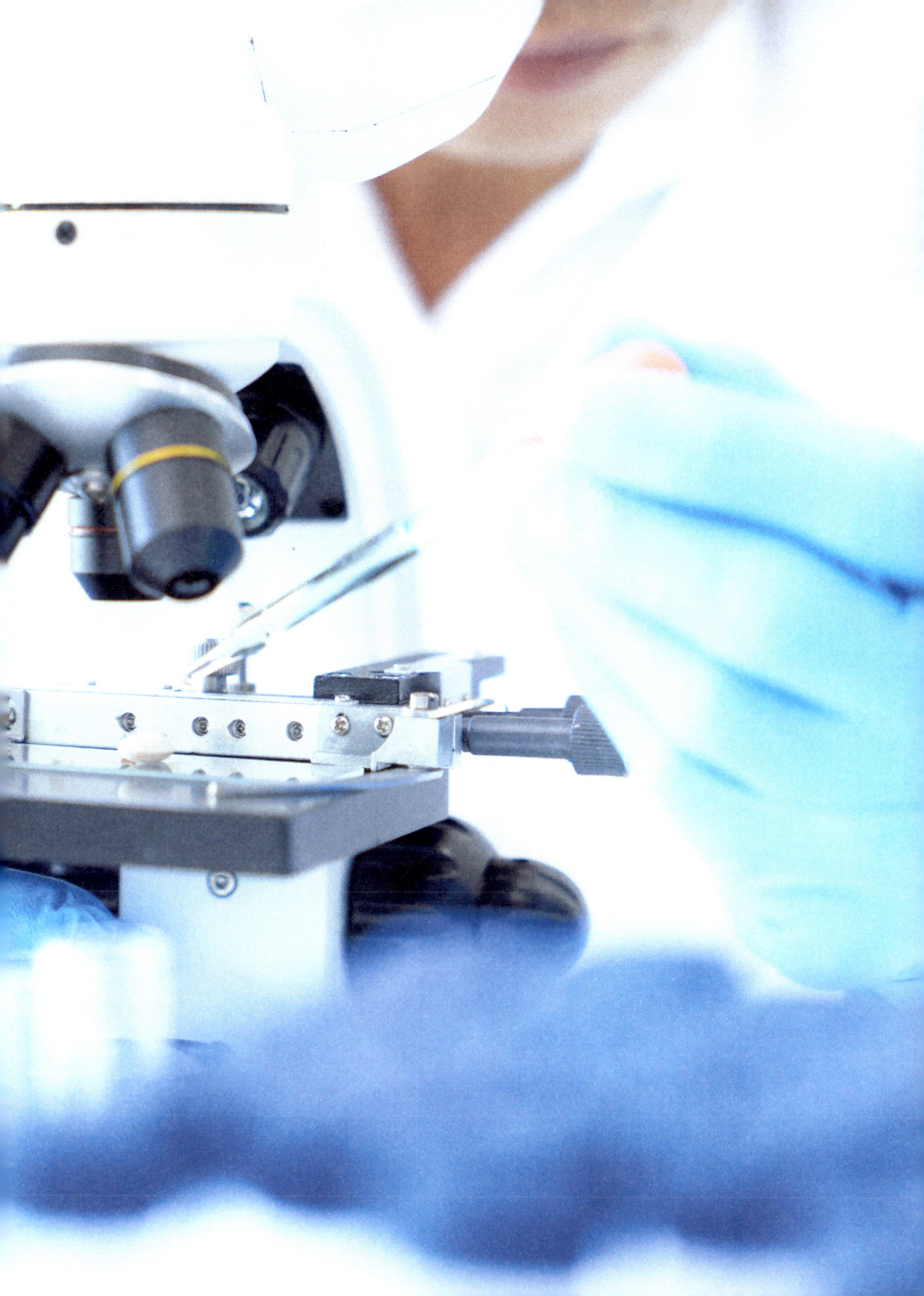

WHAT IS SCIENCE?

Science is how we explore and understand the world around us. Scientists ask questions, carry out experiments, look closely at things to see how they behave or react, and then try to make sense of what they discover!

Chemistry

Chemistry is the study of matter – the stuff that everything in the universe is made of, from the socks on your feet to the stars in space. Chemists explore what matter is made of and how it behaves in different environments and conditions.

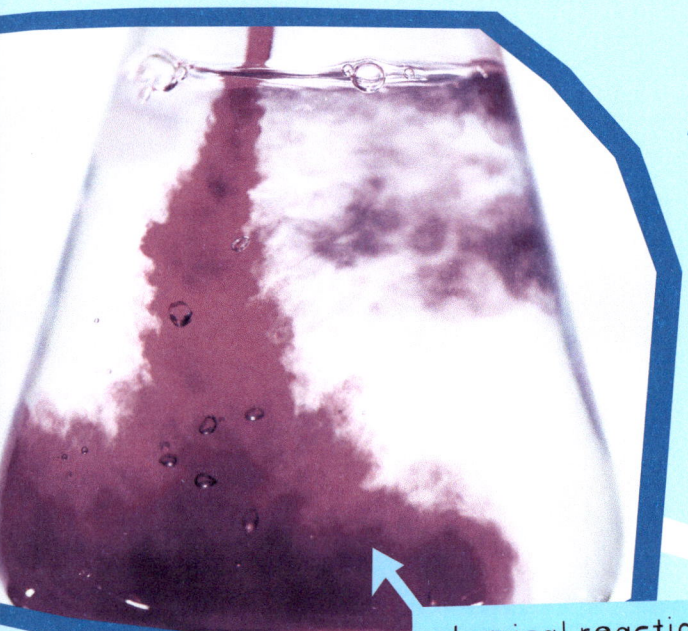

chemical reaction in progress

Physics

Have you ever wondered what electricity is, or why things fall to the ground when you drop them? To answer questions like that, you need to understand physics. Physics is the study of how the world works and how objects, forces and energy interact all around us.

Biology

Biology is the study of living things, including plants, animals and people. Biology explains how your body works, how plants and animals grow, and how all life on Earth is connected.

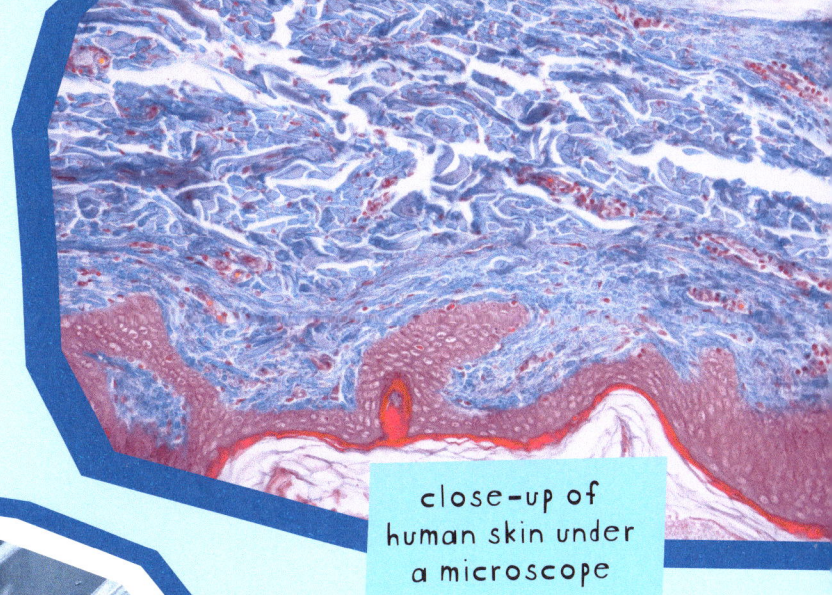

close-up of human skin under a microscope

robot producing batteries

Technology

Chemistry, physics and biology are natural sciences. Technology isn't a science in the same way, but it's difficult to separate science from technology because one leads to the other. Technology is the result of applying science to make things that can perform tasks or solve problems.

FASCINATING FACT

Science doesn't stop at chemistry, physics and biology – there are lots of other branches of science. For example, geology is the study of Earth's structure and what it's made of. Astronomy is the study of the universe and everything in it. What other sciences do you know of?

STATES OF MATTER

Chemistry is the study of matter, and everything is made of matter – but it all looks, feels and behaves differently. One reason for that is because matter comes in four different states: solid, liquid, gas and plasma.

Solid

In a solid, such as rock or ice, the particles are packed closely together so they can't move around much. That's why solids keep their shape and their volume – the amount of space they take up.

Liquid

In a liquid, such as water, juice or milk, the particles are close together but there's enough room for them to slide around. Liquids can flow, so they take the shape of the container that they're in. Although they can change shape, the volume of a liquid stays the same.

Gas

In a gas, such as air, the gas some people use for cooking, or the helium in a party balloon, the particles are spread out, so they have no fixed shape. The particles can move freely, so gases expand to fill whatever space they're in.

Plasma

The fourth state of matter – and the most unusual – is plasma. This is created when natural gas gets so hot that some of its electrons break free from their atoms or molecules (see more about atoms and molecules on pp.12–15). Plasma is found in things like the stars and lightning.

FASCINATING FACT

Solid water (ice) is less dense than liquid water, which is why icebergs float instead of sinking to the bottom of the sea!

ATOMS

All matter is made up of atoms. These tiny particles are the building blocks of everything on Earth – and beyond!

Just how small *is* an atom?

Unimaginably small! They come in different types and sizes, but even the biggest ones are smaller than one millionth of a millimetre. The full stop at the end of this sentence could fit trillions of atoms inside it.

Inside an atom

Inside tiny atoms are even tinier particles called subatomic particles. Protons and neutrons are clustered close together to form the nucleus (the centre) of the atom. Electrons whiz about outside the nucleus. Protons have a positive electrical charge. Electrons have a negative charge. Neutrons don't have an electrical charge.

Atomic maths

All chemical elements (see p.16) have their own type of atom, but in any particular type, there are always the same number of protons and electrons. The number of neutrons might be the same again, or it might be slightly different.

A lithium atom has three protons, three electrons and four neutrons.

 3 electrons 3 protons 4 neutrons

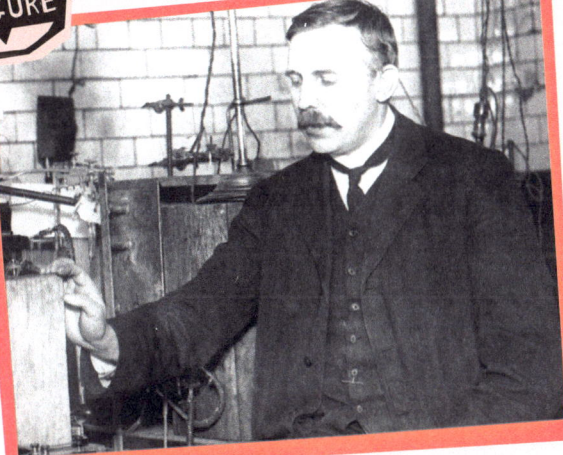

FAMOUS FIGURE

Ernest Rutherford

Until the 1890s, nobody knew about subatomic particles. After the electron was discovered in 1897, Ernest Rutherford (1871–1937) did experiments to find out more about atoms. He discovered that they were mostly empty space, but that they had a nucleus that contained most of their mass because of the protons in it. Rutherford's work was very important in understanding the structure of atoms.

Splitting the atom

When the nucleus of an atom is split, it releases a huge amount of energy in the form of heat and light. This process is called nuclear fission. Fission can generate nuclear energy, but it's also how atomic bombs work.

MOLECULES

Everything is built from particles of one sort or another. Sometimes, the particles are individual atoms or ions (atoms that are electrically charged). In other substances, the particles are made of groups of atoms called molecules.

Bonding together

In a molecule, two or more atoms are joined together by chemical bonds called covalent bonds. In this kind of bond, the atoms in the molecule share one or more pairs of electrons.

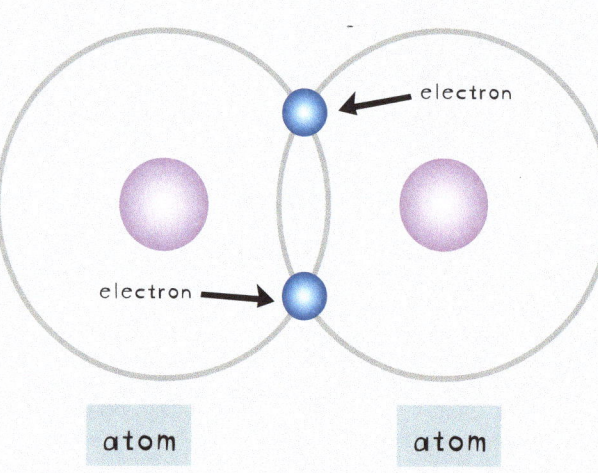

Madam C.J. Walker
FAMOUS FIGURE

In the early 1900s, Sarah Breedlove Walker became famous for using her knowledge of chemistry formulas to invent beauty products. Her creations helped many soothe dry skin and straighten their hair! She became known as Madam C.J. Walker and created her very own cosmetics company.

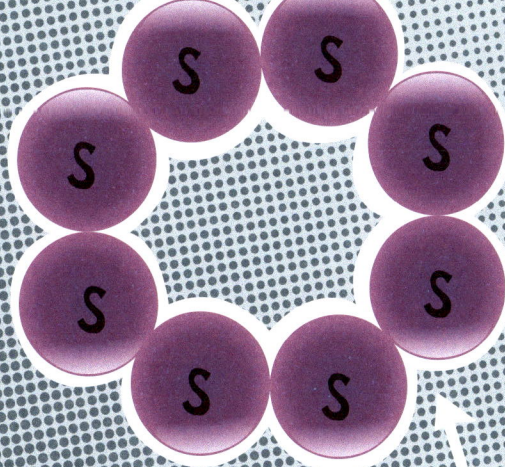

Helium (He) is a single atom.

A hydrogen (H₂) molecule is made up of two hydrogen atoms.

Elemental molecules

Some elements, like helium, don't form bonds – they are just single atoms. Others, like hydrogen and sulphur, are elemental molecules. That means they contain more than one atom bonded together.

A sulphur (S₈) molecule is made up of eight sulphur atoms, arranged in a ring structure.

Compounds

A compound is a substance made up of two or more different chemical elements that are chemically combined together. Compounds are usually molecules. For example, water is a compound – every water molecule is made up of two hydrogen atoms bonded with one oxygen atom.

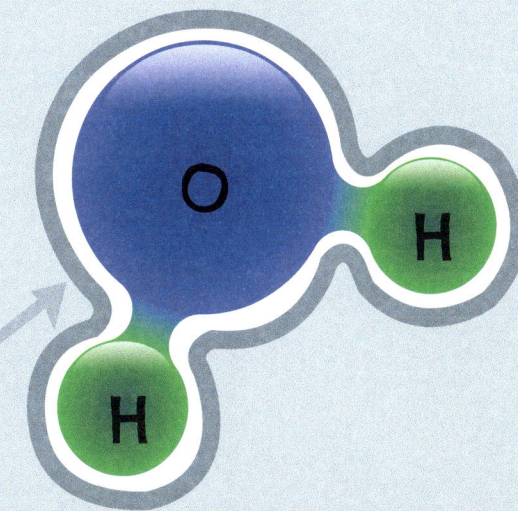

A water molecule – symbol H₂O.

TRUE OR FALSE? Molecules can be different shapes, including spirals and pyramids.

Find out on p.88!

THE PERIODIC TABLE

Chemical elements are the simplest substances that exist. Elements are pure because they're made of only one type of atom. We know of 118 elements, but we also know that there are more out there that haven't been found yet!

Charting the elements

In the 1800s, scientists began to discover many elements that they hadn't known about before. To keep track of them all, a scientist called Dmitri Mendeleev created the periodic table, which arranges the chemical elements from lowest to highest atomic number (the atomic number is in the top left-hand corner of each box). Each element has its own box, with a symbol that indicates its name, such as H for hydrogen.

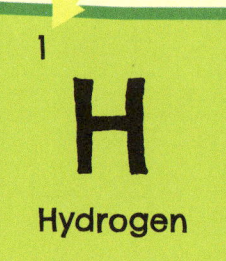

atomic number

1
H
Hydrogen

Element discoveries

9000 BC
Copper (Cu) is the first metal that humans mine and use.

1600 BC
Strange semi-metal antimony (Sb) is discovered.

1766
Henry Cavendish confirms that hydrogen gas (H) is an element.

2000 BC
Sulphur (S) is used by the ancient Egyptians to treat skin conditions.

1669
Phosphorus (P) is the first element to be discovered since ancient times.

Periodic table of elements

Group 0: the noble gases →

1 H Hydrogen																	2 He Helium
3 Li Lithium	4 Be Beryllium											5 B Boron	6 C Carbon	7 N Nitrogen	8 O Oxygen	9 F Fluorine	10 Ne Neon
11 Na Sodium	12 Mg Magnesium											13 Al Aluminium	14 Si Silicon	15 P Phosphorus	16 S Sulfur	17 Cl Chlorine	18 Ar Argon
19 K Potassium	20 Ca Calcium	21 Sc Scandium	22 Ti Titanium	23 V Vanadium	24 Cr Chromium	25 Mn Manganese	26 Fe Iron	27 Co Cobalt	28 Ni Nickel	29 Cu Copper	30 Zn Zinc	31 Ga Gallium	32 Ge Germanium	33 As Arsenic	34 Se Selenium	35 Br Bromine	36 Kr Krypton
37 Rb Rubidium	38 Sr Strontium	39 Y Yttrium	40 Zr Zirconium	41 Nb Niobium	42 Mo Molybdenum	43 Tc Technetium	44 Ru Ruthenium	45 Rh Rhodium	46 Pd Palladium	47 Ag Silver	48 Cd Cadmium	49 In Indium	50 Sn Tin	51 Sb Antimony	52 Te Tellurium	53 I Iodine	54 Xe Xenon
55 Cs Caesium	56 Ba Barium	57 La* Lanthanum	72 Hf Hafnium	73 Ta Tantalum	74 W Tungsten	75 Re Rhenium	76 Os Osmium	77 Ir Iridium	78 Pt Platinum	79 Au Gold	80 Hg Mercury	81 Tl Thallium	82 Pb Lead	83 Bi Bismuth	84 Po Polonium	85 At Astatine	86 Rn Radon
87 Fr Francium	88 Ra Radium	89 Ac** Actinium	104 Rf Rutherfordium	105 Db Dubnium	106 Sg Seaborgium	107 Bh Bohrium	108 Hs Hassium	109 Mt Meitnerium	110 Ds Darmstadtium	111 Rg Roentgenium	112 Cn Copernicium	113 Nh Nihonium	114 Fl Flerovium	115 Mc Moscovium	116 Lv Livermorium	117 Ts Tennessine	118 Og Oganesson

← Group 1: the alkali metals

*	58 Ce Cerium	59 Pr Praseodymium	60 Nd Neodymium	61 Pm Promethium	62 Sm Samarium	63 Eu Europium	64 Gd Gadolinium	65 Tb Terbium	66 Dy Dysprosium	67 Ho Holmium	68 Er Erbium	69 Tm Thulium	70 Yb Ytterbium	71 Lu Lutetium
**	90 Th Thorium	91 Pa Protactinium	92 U Uranium	93 Np Neptunium	94 Pu Plutonium	95 Am Americium	96 Cm Curium	97 Bk Berkelium	98 Cf Californium	99 Es Einsteinium	100 Fm Fermium	101 Md Mendelevium	102 No Nobelium	103 Lr Lawrencium

Groups and periods

Elements with similar properties and that behave in similar ways are positioned in vertical columns called groups. Some groups have special names. For example, Group 1 – the left-hand column – is the alkali metals. Group 0 – the far right-hand column – is the noble gases. The rows in the table are called periods.

1808
Calcium (Ca) is separated from calcium compounds and recognised as an element.

1969
Rutherfordium (Rf), named after Ernest Rutherford, is the first 'super-heavy' element to be found.

1791
The super-strong metal titanium (Ti) is discovered.

1898
Famous scientists Pierre and Marie Curie discover two new radioactive elements: radium (Ra) and polonium (Po).

2010
The most recent element to be discovered, Tennessine (Ts), is made in a laboratory.

Name that...

CHEMICAL ELEMENT

See if you can identify these chemical elements. Can you name something that each one is used for? Check your answers on p.88.

1

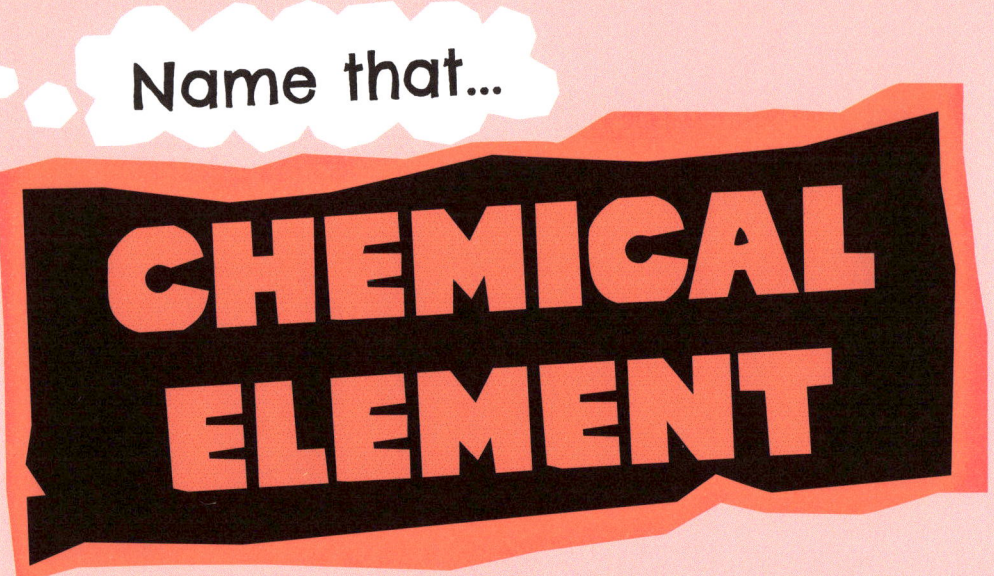

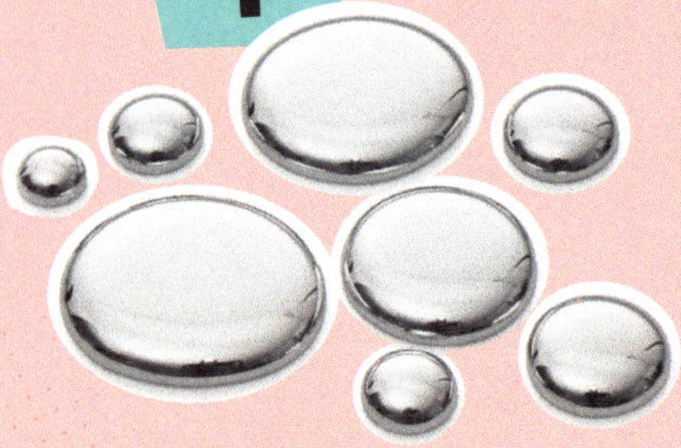

2

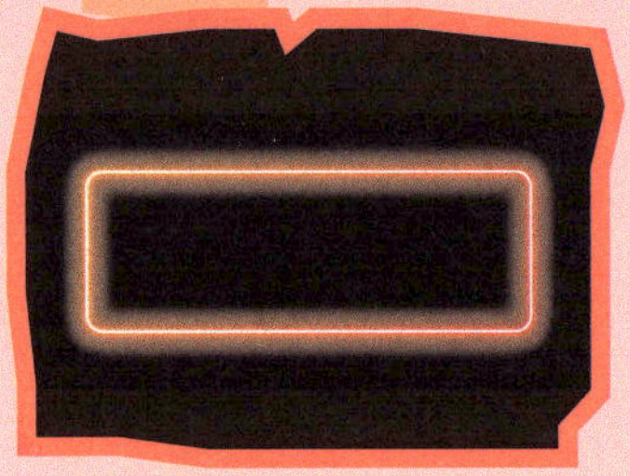

3

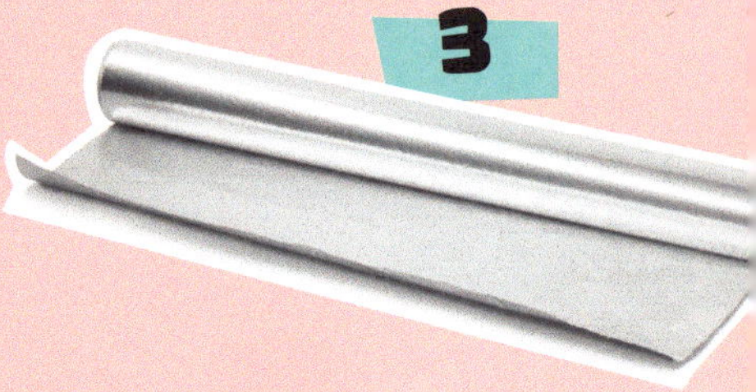

4

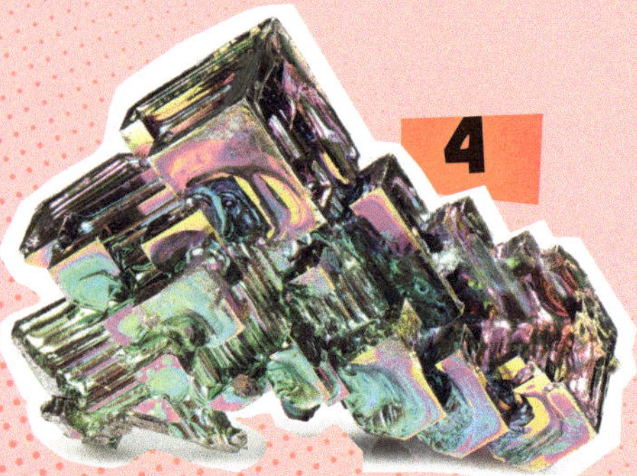

5

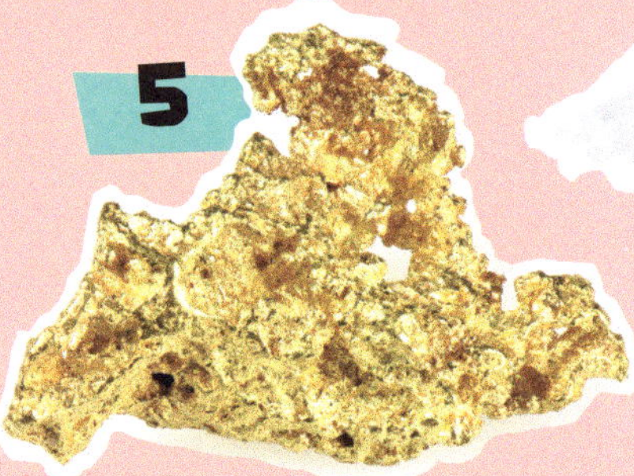

6

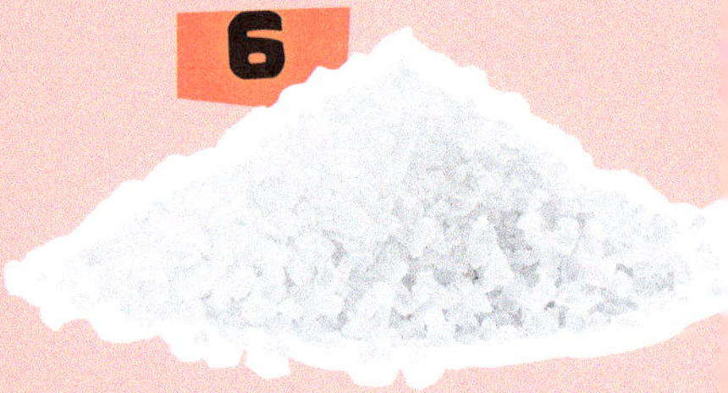

7

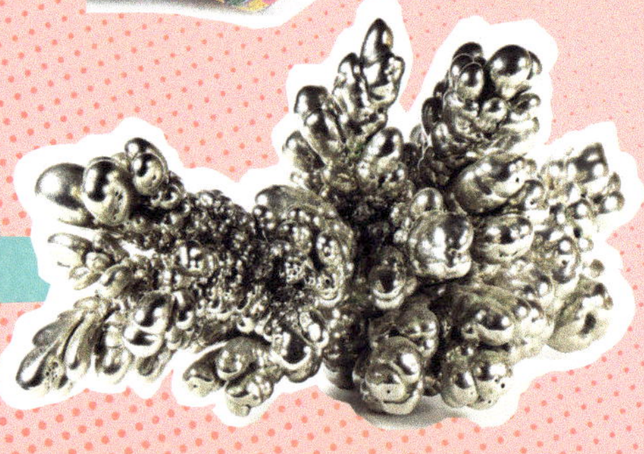

8

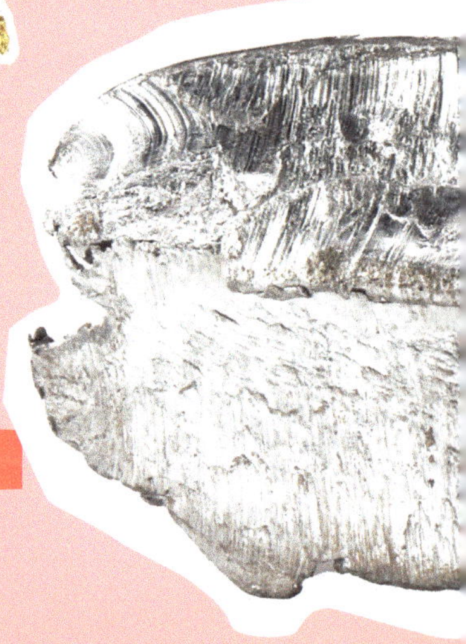

CARBON

Carbon is an incredible element. It's in everything around you – in your body, in plants and animals, in the air that you breathe, and even in space.

Carbon bonding

Carbon is special because it can form bonds in strong chains, with itself and with other elements. For example, when carbon and oxygen atoms bond, they create the gas carbon dioxide (CO_2), which plants need to make food.

Atomic arrangements

Carbon is also unusual because it forms different materials depending on how the atoms are arranged. When the atoms bond in a pyramid of layers, they create diamond – the hardest natural substance on Earth. Carbon atoms arranged in thin, flat sheets form graphite, which is soft enough to put in pencils.

FASCINATING FACT

In diamond, each carbon atom is bonded to four other carbon atoms, creating a crystal structure.

Buckyballs

Buckminsterfullerene – buckyballs for short – is a type of carbon. A buckyball is basically a hollow molecule made up of 60 carbon atoms in the shape of a football! Scientists are exploring ways to use the strong structure of buckyballs in things like medicine and electronics.

Born in space

Carbon comes from stars. Very old stars get incredibly hot inside. Under intense heat and pressure, smaller atoms fuse together to form carbon atoms. If a star dies in a supernova explosion, the carbon atoms are shot out into space. Over time, they become parts of new stars, planets and even life on Earth.

METALS

Of the 118 known chemical elements, more than 90 of them are metals. You probably think of metals as being strong, heavy solids. And some of them are! But they're not all the same.

Properties of metals

Most metals are a silver or grey colour – only copper and gold stand out with different colours. Metals are also usually malleable, which means they can be bent and shaped without breaking.

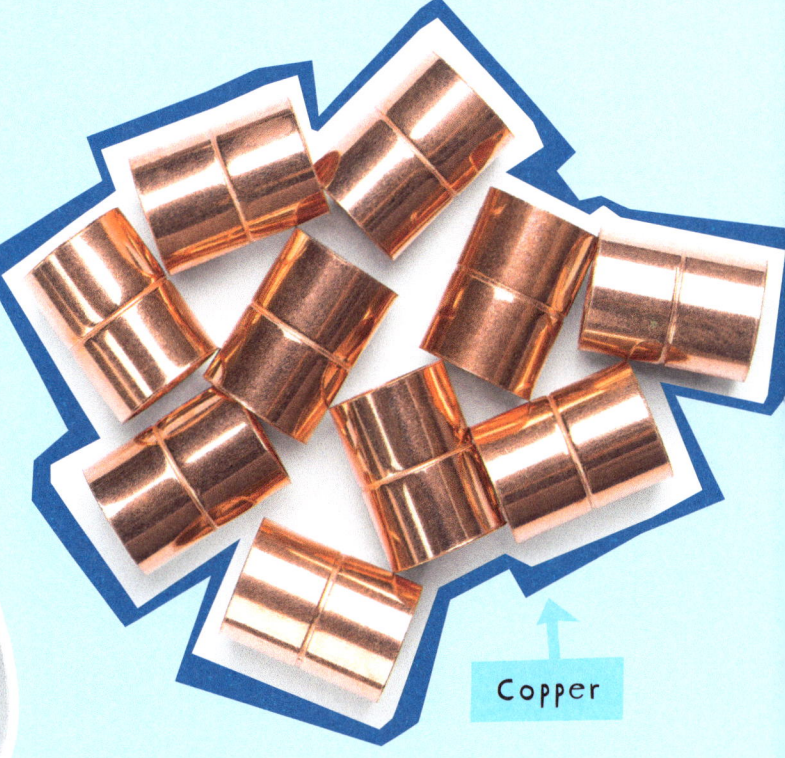

Copper

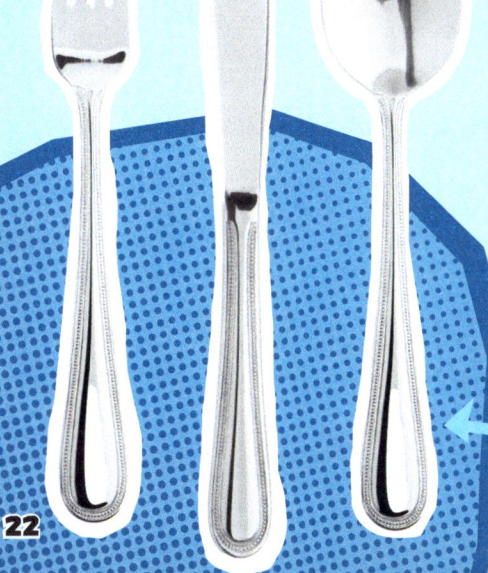

Alloys

Alloys are new metals that are made by mixing two or more metal elements. Bronze is an alloy of copper and tin. Stainless steel is an alloy of iron and chromium.

stainless steel

Good conductors

In metals, the shared electrons can move between atoms. That's why metals are good conductors of electricity – because an electric current is a moving stream of electrons.

Alkali metals

The alkali metals, like lithium, sodium and potassium, are so soft that you can cut them with a knife. They also have strong reactions when mixed with other substances. For example, they'll catch fire in water. Drop a piece of francium in water and the francium blows apart in a very dangerous reaction. You should never try to do this at home.

Stand back!

Mining metals

Most metals come from ores. These are metals combined with other elements in the ground, such as iron ore. To get pure metal, the ore has to be dug out of the ground and separated from the other elements.

TRUE OR FALSE? Mercury is the only metal that is a liquid at room temperature. Find out on p.88!

Super Stats

METALS

Metals are everywhere on Earth and we use them in lots of different ways. But you might find some of these metallic facts and statistics surprising!

Seas of gold

Scientists think that there's around 20 million tonnes of gold dissolved in the Earth's oceans. Unfortunately, it's so diluted that it's almost impossible to extract it.

Precious metal

Platinum is 30 times rarer than gold, making it one of the most scarce precious metals on the planet.

Best recycler

Aluminium can be easily recycled over and over again. Nearly 75% of all the aluminium that has ever been mined is still in use.

Growing iron

Iron expands when it gets hot, so structures made of iron 'grow' in the summer. The Eiffel Tower can be 15 centimetres taller in the summer than in the winter!

Melting metals

It takes a high heat to melt most metals, but gallium's melting point is only 29º Celsius. That means it can melt in your hand.

Reflections

Silver is the most reflective metal. It can bounce back 95% of light, which is why it's great for making mirrors!

Heavy metal

The heaviest metal that occurs naturally (that is, one that's not made by scientists) is osmium. It's nearly twice as dense as lead.

Strong but light

Titanium is generally as strong as steel, but it is 45% lighter. That's why titanium is used for things like aeroplanes and spacecraft.

Top 5 toxic metals

1. Arsenic
2. Cadmium
3. Chromium
4. Lead
5. Mercury

CHEMICAL REACTIONS

When two or more chemical elements are put together, they may react with each other to create a new substance. Think of it like making a cake – the different ingredients combine to make something new.

What happens?

When elements combine, the bonds between some atoms break and new bonds can form. The number of atoms doesn't change, but they're rearranged to create a different structure with different properties.

How do you know?

You can often tell when a chemical reaction has taken place just by looking at the substances. Has something changed colour? Has it got hotter or colder? Can you see bubbles or a gas escaping? Those are all evidence of a reaction.

Put a mint in a bottle of fizzy drink and you'll see a chemical reaction!
WARNING: Don't try this indoors!

rust, or iron oxide

Metal reactions

Some metals are very unreactive: gold will stay shiny for hundreds of years, for example. Other metals tarnish (their surface goes dull). Iron can form iron oxide – rust. This is caused by a chemical reaction between the iron, water and the oxygen in air.

Awesome equations

Scientists show what happens in a chemical reaction using an equation. For example, the equation for the reaction that creates carbon dioxide (see p.20) is:

$$\text{carbon} + \text{oxygen} = \text{carbon dioxide}$$
$$C + O_2 = CO_2$$

The second line shows how the equation is written in chemical symbols.

FASCINATING FACT

You can speed up a chemical reaction by adding energy, such as heat, sunlight or electricity.

ACIDS AND ALKALIS

Acids and alkalis are two groups of chemicals that are almost opposites. They react in different ways and have special properties that make them very useful in everyday life.

Natural acids

Some acids occur naturally. There's acid in fruit like lemons, limes and oranges, for example, and in vinegar. And amazing ants make an acid called formic acid, which they squirt at their enemies!

Other acids

You can eat oranges and put vinegar on your chips without worrying because the acid in them isn't harmful. But some acids, such as hydrochloric acid and sulphuric acid, are made in laboratories. These are stronger and more dangerous. Scientists have to be very careful when handling them.

Alkalis

Alkalis are found in things like soap and baking soda. They're often bitter or slippery. Alkalis are brilliant at breaking down grease, so they're great as cleaning products!

The pH scale

Scientists use the pH scale to measure how acidic or alkaline something is. The scale runs from 0 to 14. Numbers below 7 are acid and above 7 are alkali. pH7 is neutral. What number on the scale do you think lemon juice would be?

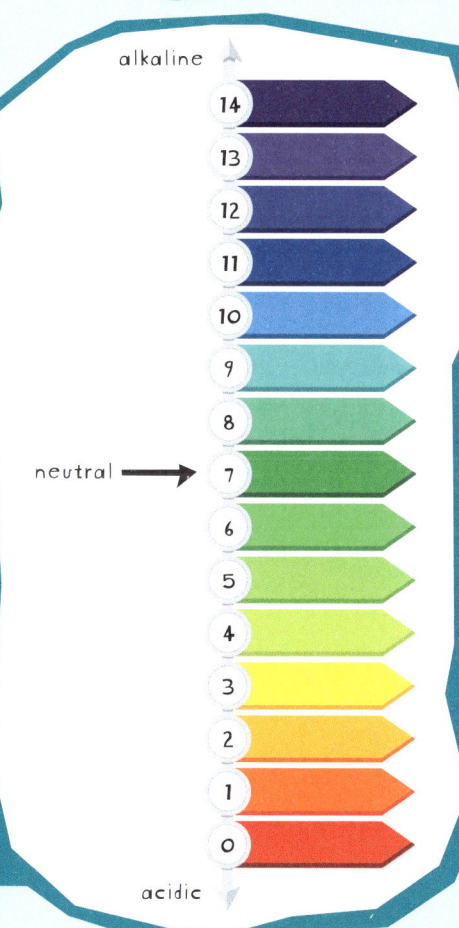

TRUE OR FALSE? If you mix an acid with an alkali, the reaction results in an acid. Find out on p.88!

MATERIALS

Take a look around you. From the clothes you're wearing to the book you're holding, to the building you're sitting in – everything is made of materials.

Hands off my coat!

Natural materials

Natural materials can come from living (organic) things, such as wood from trees or wool from sheep. They can also come from inorganic things like rocks and minerals. Raw materials are natural materials that are turned into human-made ones. For example, steel comes from the raw materials iron and carbon.

Human-made materials

Scientists can create all sorts of materials that don't occur naturally. Plastic, synthetic rubber, manufactured glass, synthetic fabrics and ceramics are all examples of human-made materials. They can be made into just about any item you need!

The right material for the job

Different materials have different properties. They can be light or heavy, soft or hard, smooth or rough, flexible or rigid. A material's properties determine what it can be used for. After all, you wouldn't build a house out of paper or make a coat out of rock!

Fantastic plastic?

Plastic is a brilliant material. It's cheap to make, as well as being strong, light and long-lasting. These properties also cause problems, though. Some plastic can be recycled, but the rest is buried in landfill where it takes hundreds of years to break down.

TRUE OR FALSE? Glass is made out of the raw material sand. Find out on p.88!

Name that... MATERIAL

See if you can identify these materials (not the objects!). Roll over to p.89 to see if you got them all right.

1

2

3

4

5

THE SCIENCE OF WEATHER

The study of the weather is a type of science called meteorology. Scientists look at what's happening in Earth's atmosphere to predict what kind of weather is on the way, from sunshine to snowstorms.

What is weather?

The weather is a huge, constantly changing system where the Sun, air and water all interact. Different types of weather come from different combinations of these things.

Air pressure

The Sun heats up our planet, but different areas heat up at different rates. For example, land heats up more quickly than water. This forms warm and cool areas, which creates differences in air pressure. And air pressure helps determine what the weather will be like.

Rising air and falling rain

Warm air rises. As it does, cooler air rushes in beneath it, which creates wind. The rising warm air also carries water vapour from lakes and seas up into the atmosphere. Eventually this forms clouds and, when they get heavy enough, the moisture falls as rain.

Stormy weather

Lightning is basically a huge spark of electricity in the atmosphere between clouds, the air or the ground. It's caused by particles in clouds bumping into each other, creating a build-up of electric charge. The bottom of the cloud becomes negatively charged, and the positive charge of the ground is pulled towards the negative charge until they meet and a streak of lightning is released.

Thunder is the sound that the lightning creates; we hear thunder after we see the lightning flash because light travels faster than sound.

FASCINATING FACT

About one billion tonnes of rain falls on Earth every single minute.

QUIZ YOURSELF ON...

CHEMISTRY

What's your reaction to a quiz on chemistry? See how much you've learnt here!

1 Which of these is not one of the states of matter?

A. plasma

B. element

C. liquid

2 Which particle has a positive charge?

A. proton

B. neutron

C. electron

Check your answers on p.89!

3 How many atoms are there in a hydrogen molecule?

A. one

B. two

C. three

4 Which element has the symbol Cu?

A. carbon

B. chlorine

C. copper

TRUE OR FALSE? Metals do not conduct electricity very well.

Find out on p.88!

5 Which of these is a type of carbon?

- **A.** lead
- **B.** bronze
- **C.** graphite

6 Which of these is a common property of metals?

- **A.** malleable
- **B.** rough
- **C.** transparent

7 What is an alloy?

- **A.** a subatomic particle
- **B.** a mixture of two or more metals
- **C.** a type of acid

8 What number is an alkali on the pH scale?

- **A.** above 7
- **B.** 7
- **C.** below 7

9 Which of these is a natural material?

- **A.** synthetic fabric
- **B.** plastic
- **C.** wood

10 What is the science of weather called?

- **A.** weatherology
- **B.** meteorology
- **C.** climatology

WHAT IS ENERGY?

Physics explores how objects, forces and energy interact all around us. Energy is the ability to do work or to make things change in some way. From riding bikes to launching rockets, energy is what makes things happen.

Movement

You need energy to do anything. For example, when playing a sport, you're using energy to run, jump and kick. You get that energy from the food you eat, which comes from plants or animals. They in turn get their energy from sunlight.

Transport

Machines and vehicles are powered by fuel, which is a source of energy. They move us from place to place, make tools work and do the heavy lifting that we wouldn't have enough energy to do on our own.

Light and heat

Energy isn't just about movement. It's also what creates heat and light. Light bulbs and stoves both use electrical energy. Computers and smartphones also use this kind of energy to connect to the internet, store data and stay on!

Energy is always there

An amazing thing about energy is that it's never lost – it just changes form. When you jump on a trampoline, your energy of movement (kinetic energy) is temporarily turned into stored (potential) energy as you rise up in the air. That energy is then turned back into kinetic energy as you fall back down!

FASCINATING FACT

If you're active, you use about as much energy every day as a 100-watt light bulb! Even when you're asleep, your body is using energy to breathe, digest food and keep you warm.

ENERGY SOURCES

We need lots of energy to fuel our world. This comes from several different sources, which create energy in different ways.

Fossil fuels

Coal, oil and natural gas are called fossil fuels because they are formed from the remains of ancient plants and animals. Burning these fuels generates energy. The problem with fossil fuels is that they're non-renewable. That means that we're using them up faster than they can be replaced, so eventually they will run out.

A 'nodding donkey' pumps oil from underground.

Renewable resources

We can create energy from other sources. These will never run out, so they're known as renewable resources.

Solar panels capture sunlight and convert it into electricity through special cells called photovoltaic (PV) cells.

Wind power works by using turbines to capture wind energy. The wind spins the turbine blades, which drive a generator to produce electricity.

Hydroelectricity also works by spinning turbines connected to a generator, but the turbines are turned by flowing water instead of wind.

Tidal power captures energy from the ocean tides, using underwater turbines driven by rising and falling water.

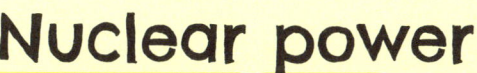

Nuclear power

Nuclear power begins by splitting atoms in a reactor. This releases heat that turns water into steam, which spins turbines to produce electricity. Nuclear fuels aren't renewable, but only small amounts are needed to create lots of energy, so they will last longer.

LIGHT AND COLOUR

Light is essential to all life on Earth. Without it, there would be no plants and no animals – including humans!

Sources of light

Light comes from different sources. Some, such as the Sun, lightning and fire, are natural sources. But humans have also learnt how to make their own light sources – for example, torches, candles and lamps.

Sunlight...

Our main source of light is the Sun, which emits light in all directions. Although the Sun is around 148 million kilometres from Earth, sunlight reaches us in just 8 minutes and 20 seconds!

...and shadows

When sunlight is blocked by an opaque object – like you! – a dark shape forms. That's a shadow. Shadows are the same shape as the object blocking the Sun, but they may look stretched out or squashed down depending on the angle of the sunlight.

Electromagnetic spectrum

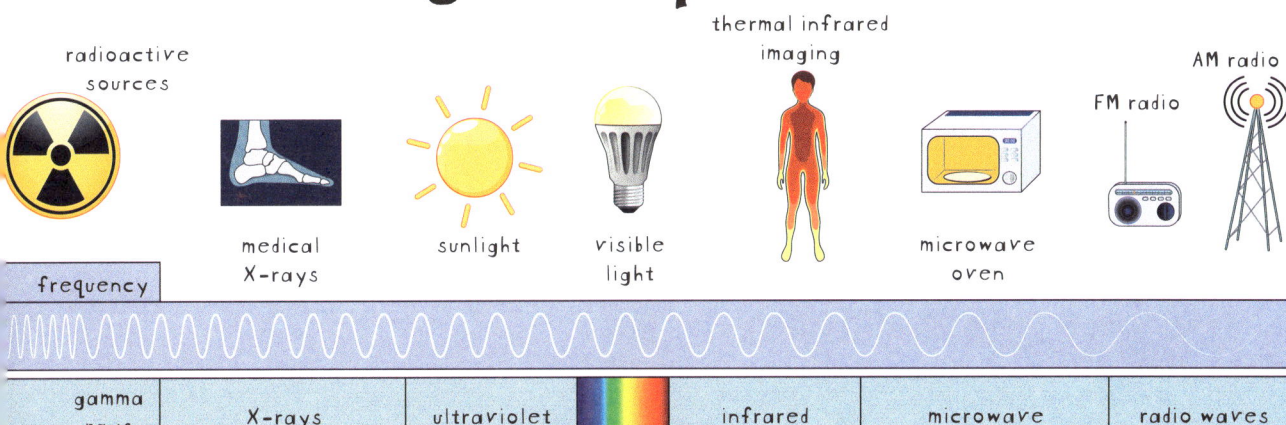

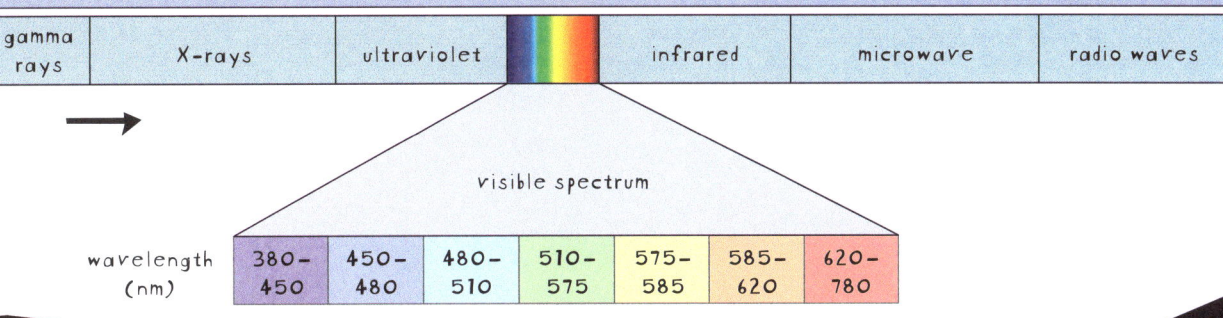

Electromagnetic spectrum

There are different types of light, which sit on a scale called the electromagnetic spectrum. They're organised in order of their wavelength. Radio waves have the longest wavelengths, then microwaves, infrared, visible light, ultraviolet, X-rays and gamma rays, which have the shortest wavelength. The only type of light we can see is visible light.

Splitting light

Visible light looks white, but it's really made up of different colours. You can see these colours by splitting white light through a glass object called a prism. You also see them when light shines through raindrops to form a rainbow.

ZOOM IN

White light is made up of red, orange, yellow, green, blue, indigo and violet light.

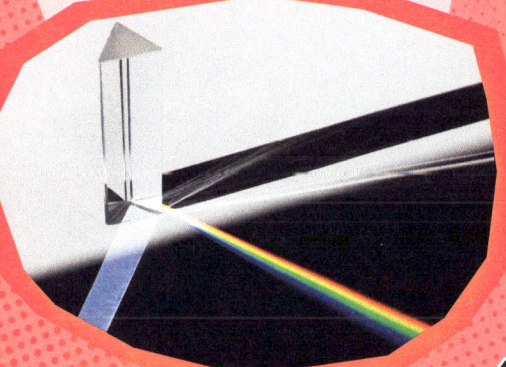

REFLECTION AND REFRACTION

When light hits an object, different things can happen. If the object is completely transparent, the light will pass straight through it, almost as if it wasn't there. But sometimes other things happen.

Are you seeing things?

Most objects don't make their own light – they reflect light from other sources. Light bounces off the object and enters our eyes, and that's how we see things. In the dark, the opening in the middle of the eye, the pupil, gets bigger to let in more light.

FASCINATING FACT

The Moon looks bright in the night sky, but it doesn't make its own light. That brightness you see is the Moon reflecting light from the Sun.

Reflective objects

When light can't pass through an object, it usually reflects off it. A reflection looks the same as the real object but back to front. Left becomes right and vice versa.

When the light bounces off a smooth surface like glass or a mirror evenly, you get a clear reflection.

If the surface is rougher, such as water with ripples in it, the reflection will be slightly distorted.

Bending light

Light usually travels in straight lines. But when it passes from one material to another, it might bend, or refract. Refraction happens because light travels at different speeds through different materials. For example, it travels faster through air than it does through water.

ELECTRICITY

Electricity is a stream of tiny particles called electrons flowing through a metal conductor. It's the type of energy used to power lights and all sorts of household gadgets.

Conductors and insulators

Some metals conduct electricity well – electricity flows through them easily. Other materials like plastic, known as insulators, don't conduct electricity. Electrical wires that carry electricity are often covered in plastic, so you don't get an electric shock when you touch them.

Electrical circuits

An electrical circuit is a closed path, or loop, that electricity can flow through. A circuit usually has a power source, like a battery, as well as wires and other components like bulbs or motors. When the circuit is closed (connected), electricity flows through it. When it's open, the electrical flow stops.

FAMOUS FIGURE

Thomas Edison

Thomas Edison (1847–1931) was an amazing inventor. He was fascinated by electricity and tried to find ways that it could be put to good use. Edison helped to design the first practical electric light bulb. His Electric Light Company set up power stations, which made electricity available to homes and businesses for the first time.

Static electricity

An electrical charge can build up on the surface of an object. This is called static electricity because the charge stays in one place instead of flowing. It's caused by friction (see p.54) between two insulating materials.

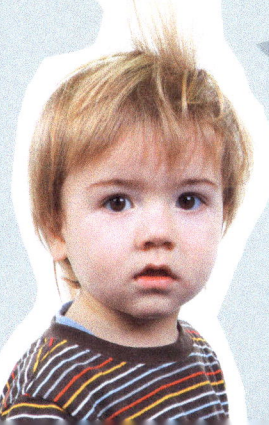

If you rub a balloon against your clothes, an electric charge builds on the balloon that then attracts other things – like your hair!

47

MAGNETS

Magnetism is an amazing force that comes from magnets. A magnet is an object that pulls magnetic materials towards it.

What materials are magnetic?

The short answer is, hardly any! Plastic, paper, glass, wood – none of them will be attracted by a magnet. Not even all metals are magnetic. Aluminium, copper, silver and gold aren't. But iron is very magnetic, and any metal with iron in it, such as steel paperclips, will be attracted by a magnet.

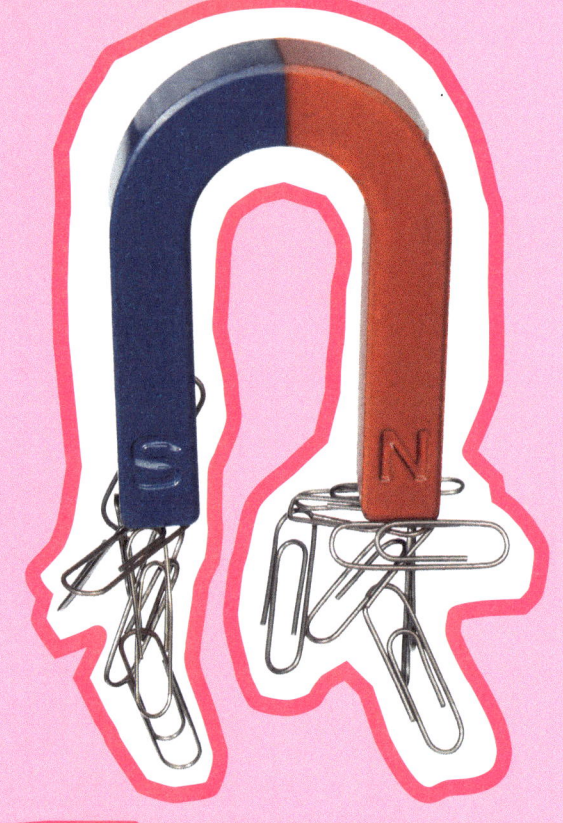

Polar opposites

At the ends of a magnet are two poles – a north pole and a south pole. The magnetic force is strongest at the poles.

Opposite poles attract each other.

The same poles repel each other.

Magnets everywhere...

You won't always be able to spot them, but magnets are used in loads of everyday things.

They keep the fridge door shut.

They help to create sound in speakers.

They start off a roller coaster and slow it down at the end.

TRUE OR FALSE? The magnetic force gets stronger the further from the magnet an object is. Find out on p.88!

49

ELECTROMAGNETISM

When you combine magnetism and electricity you get a kind of force called electromagnetism.

Electromagnets

When an electric current flows through a wire, it creates a magnetic field around it. This makes the wire act like a magnet – attracting or repelling magnetic materials. You can turn electromagnets on and off by controlling the electric current.

Electromagnets are used in medical machinery such as MRI machines.

Our magnetic planet

Earth is one huge magnet! Earth's core has lots of iron in it. When the planet spins, the metal in this giant ball of iron creates a magnetic field that moves around Earth. Magnets on Earth are affected by this magnetic field. If you dangle a magnet so it can move freely, one end will point to the North Pole and the other to the South Pole.

Earth's magnetic field

Compass points

If you've ever used a magnetic compass then you've tapped into Earth's magnetic field! The tiny magnet inside the compass is moved by the magnetic field so that it always points towards the Earth's magnetic North pole.

FASCINATING FACT

Earth's magnetic field protects the planet by deflecting (pushing away) solar winds – charged particles from the Sun.

WHAT ARE FORCES?

A force is something that acts on an object – a push or a pull. You can't see a force, but you can see the *effect* that forces have.

Making changes

Forces make objects speed up, slow down or change direction. For example, pulling may slow something down while pushing may speed it up. Forces can also change the shape of an object. Here are some examples:

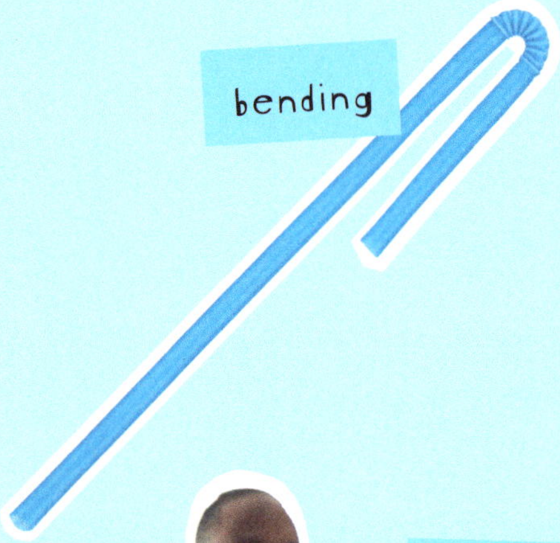

bending

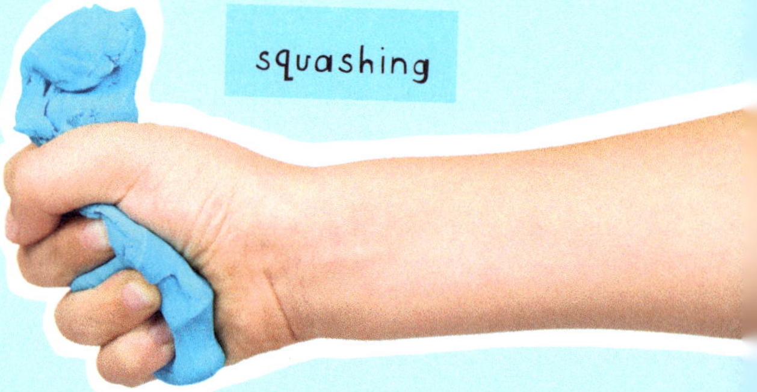

squashing

stretching

twisting

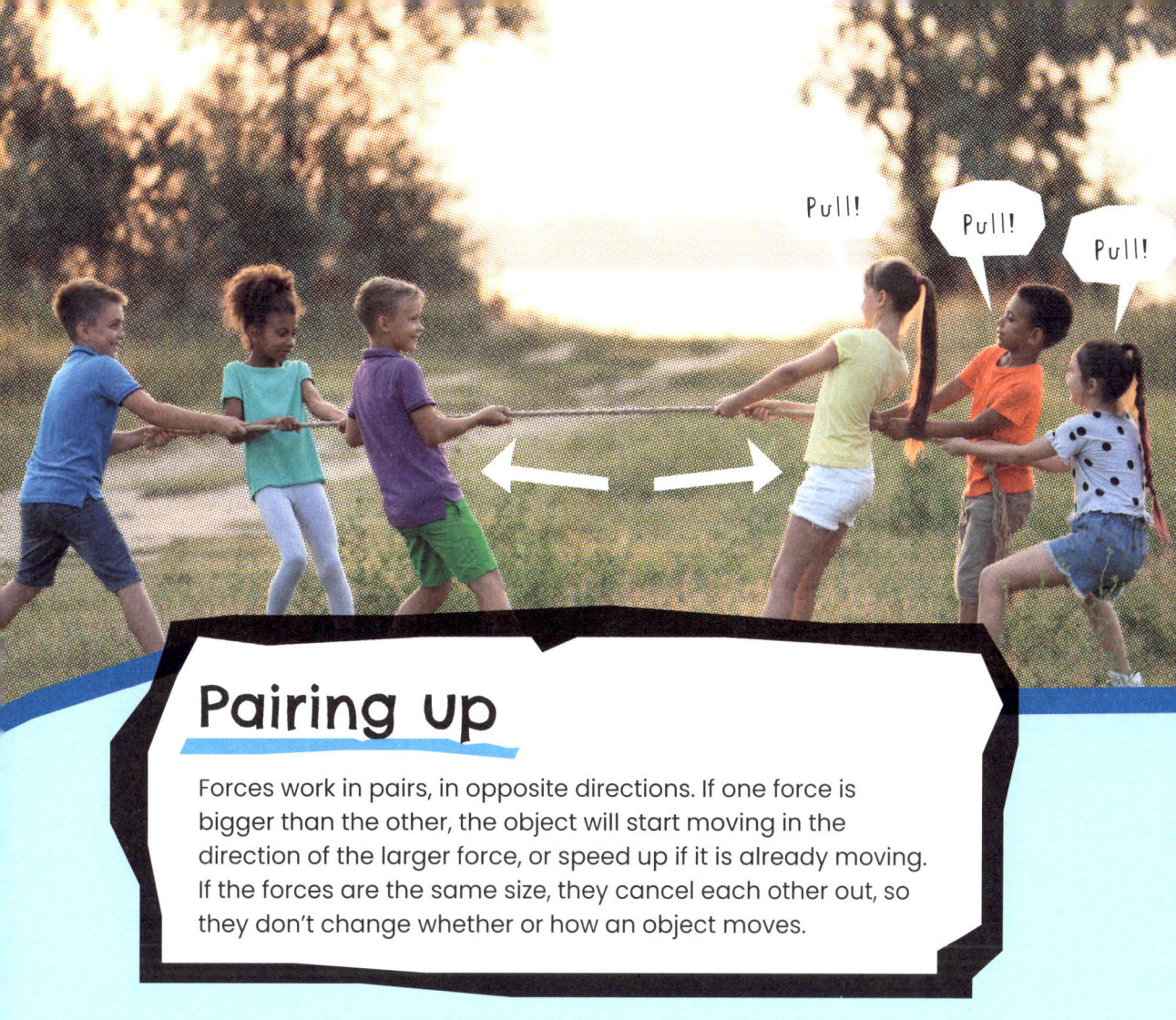

Pairing up

Forces work in pairs, in opposite directions. If one force is bigger than the other, the object will start moving in the direction of the larger force, or speed up if it is already moving. If the forces are the same size, they cancel each other out, so they don't change whether or how an object moves.

Measuring forces

The size of a force is measured in newtons (N), after the famous scientist Sir Isaac Newton, who was the first person to describe the force of gravity.

In diagrams, forces are usually represented with arrows. The tip of the arrow points in the direction of the force; the length of the arrow usually shows the strength of the force.

TRUE OR FALSE? Balanced forces will measure 0 newtons. Find out on p.88!

FRICTION AND RESISTANCE

Friction is a force that acts to slow objects down. It works on the ground, in the air and in water.

On the ground

Friction is the force that's created when two objects rub against each other. When you walk, friction is created between your shoes and the ground. Rough surfaces, like gravel, create more friction than smooth ones. That's why you're more likely to slip over on ice than you are on gravel.

Air resistance

Air resistance is a type of friction that acts on objects moving through the air. As a plane flies, air resistance pushes against the plane in the opposite direction to the way it's moving. As a parachute falls to the ground, air resistance pushes upwards, slowing its fall.

Water resistance

Friction works in water, too. When you're swimming, you can feel the force of the water pushing against you – that's water resistance slowing you down!

FASCINATING FACT

There's no air resistance in space, because there's no air!

I'm freezing!

Heating up

When two surfaces rub against each other, the friction between them creates heat. You've probably used this idea yourself, rubbing your hands together to warm yourself up!

GRAVITY

Gravity is a force of attraction – it pulls things together. Without gravity, everything in the universe would fly apart!

Small objects = weak gravity

Everything around you has gravity – this book... your pet cat... you! Even things you can't see, such as atoms, have gravity. All these objects are relatively small, though, so their gravitational pull is weak. That's why people aren't constantly being pulled together.

Big objects = strong gravity

Huge objects exert a lot of gravity. Earth's gravity pulls all the smaller objects on its surface towards its centre, which is why things fall downwards when you drop them. In space, gravity is what keeps the planets moving around the Sun, as their gravity pulls on each other.

Earth's gravity keeps your feet on the ground.

Mass and weight

Mass is how much matter (stuff) an object is made up of. Mass is measured in grams and kilograms.

Mass and weight are not the same thing. Weight is the force of gravity on an object. Because it's a force, it's measured in newtons.

Mass – not weight!

FAMOUS FIGURE: Albert Einstein

Famous physicist Albert Einstein (1879–1955) had some mind-bending ideas about gravity. He said that it wasn't just an invisible force pulling objects. Instead, he suggested that massive objects like stars and planets bend the 'fabric' of space. This makes objects 'fall' towards them, like marbles rolling towards a heavy ball on a stretchy, curved trampoline!

FASCINATING FACT

You might have heard that Sir Isaac Newton discovered the laws of gravity after an apple fell from a tree and hit him on the head! He actually first thought about gravity when he saw an apple fall from a tree, but there's no evidence that he was hit by the apple!

SPEED AND MOTION

Without forces acting on objects, everything would stay in the same place. But because forces are at work everywhere, all the time, the things around us are constantly in motion.

Let's go!

Forces can make something that is completely still start moving. For example, a swing in the park will hang straight down, but if you apply force by pushing it, it will start to move forwards and then backwards.

Speeding up

The more force you apply, the faster an object will move. This increase in speed is called acceleration. If you start running, you will feel yourself accelerating. You'll keep going until you're running as fast as you can. Then you will stay at the same speed (or slow down because you're tired).

Thrust and drag

As well as gravity, friction and air resistance, two other forces of movement are thrust and drag. Thrust powers something forward through the air. Drag works in the opposite direction, like air resistance (see p.54).

Increasing forces

Some simple machines (see p.74) are used to increase the power of certain forces. Levers increase the force of pushes and pulls. Gears make it easier to accelerate. Pulleys make it easier to lift heavy objects.

ZOOM IN

For an object like a rocket to move upwards, thrust must be greater than drag.

 Super Stats

FANTASTIC FORCES

Forces might be invisible, but they have some amazing features and effects!

The speed of gravity

Gravity pulls objects to the ground at a speed of about 9.8 metres per second squared (9.8 m/s²). This means that for every second something is falling, its speed is increasing by 9.8 metres per second.

Formula 1 facts

A Formula 1 car can accelerate from 0 to 100 kilometres per hour in about 2.6 seconds. When accelerating so quickly, these cars can generate more than five times the force of gravity (5g), which can make the drivers feel five times heavier than they really are!

 Magnetic field in space

Earth's magnetic field stretches 65,000 kilometres into space towards the Sun. That's about one-sixth of the journey to the Moon.

Strongest magnet

Scientists have created a superconducting magnet with a field strength of 20 tesla – 400,000 times stronger than Earth's magnetic field, which is 0.00005 tesla (50 microtesla).

 ## Measuring magnets

The strength of a magnet is measured in units called gauss or teslas, where 10,000 gauss = 1 tesla.

 ## Top speed

Terminal velocity is the maximum speed something can reach as it falls. For a skydiver falling in a tummy-down position, terminal velocity is about 193 kilometres per hour. But their maximum speed increases if they switch to a more streamlined pencil dive.

 ## Every second counts

Olympic swimmers shave off all their body hair and wear super-smooth swimsuits to reduce water resistance when they're racing. This tiny reduction in drag can improve their swimming speed by 2–3% – which could be the winning margin!

 ## Emergency stop

The tyres on an average car create enough friction with the road to stop a car travelling at 100 kilometres per hour in about 13–15 car lengths.

QUIZ YOURSELF ON...

PHYSICS

What do you remember about Physics? There are questions on everything from energy, to forces, to friction and magnets....

1 What is energy of movement called?

A. kinetic energy

B. potential energy

C. electrical energy

2 Which of these resources is renewable?

A. coal

B. natural gas

C. wind

Check your answers on p.89!

3 What type of light splits to form a rainbow?

A. visible light

B. infrared light

C. ultraviolet light

4 What is the 'bending' of light called?

A. conductivity

B. reflection

C. refraction

TRUE OR FALSE? Smooth surfaces create more friction than rough surfaces.

Find out on p.88!

5 Which force causes static electricity?

A. magnetism

B. friction

C. gravity

6 Where on a magnet is the magnetic force strongest?

A. in the middle

B. at the north pole

C. at both the north and south poles

7 What happens if forces acting on an object are the same size?

A. The forces cancel each other out.

B. The forces slow the object down.

C. The forces speed the object up.

8 What unit is used to measure forces?

A. kilograms

B. teslas

C. newtons

9 What does friction do to two objects?

A. pushes them apart

B. slows them down

C. makes them speed up

Thrust is…

A. a force of nature

B. a gravitational force

C. a force of movement

THE VARIETY OF LIFE

Biology is the science of living things (organisms). That includes humans, of course, but it also covers everything else on Earth that grows and moves. With more than 2.16 million known species of animal and 400,000 known species of plants, that's a lot of life!

Categories of life

Scientists split living things into groups and levels based on their characteristics. For example, organisms in a particular group might look similar or move in the same way. Each level gets more specific, grouping organisms that are more and more alike. For example, here are the levels for a grey wolf.

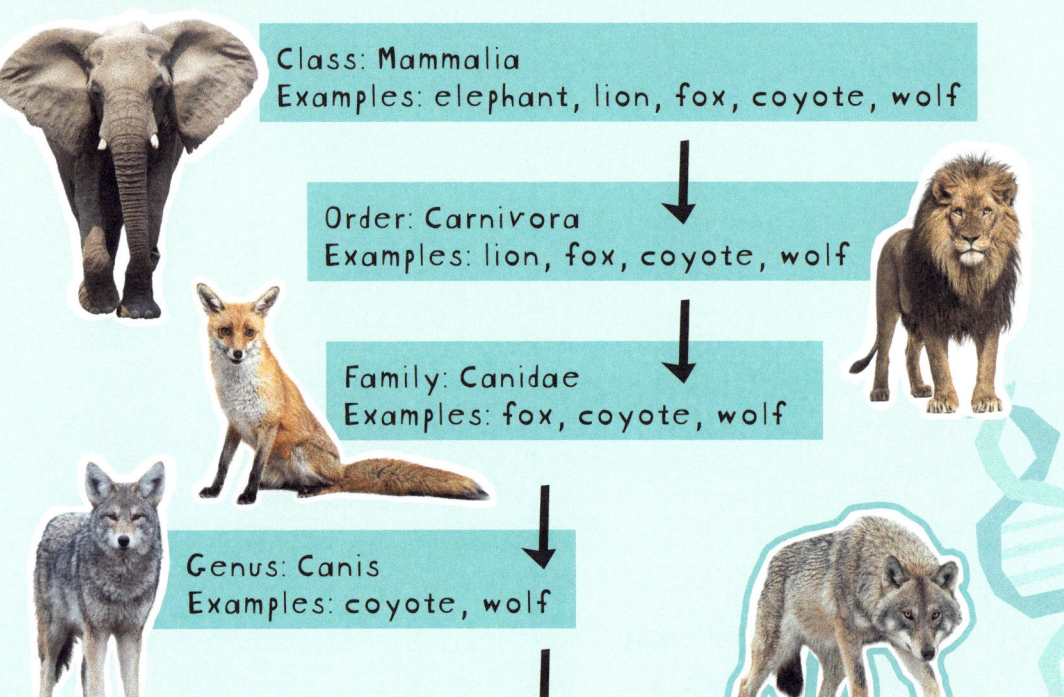

Class: Mammalia
Examples: elephant, lion, fox, coyote, wolf

Order: Carnivora
Examples: lion, fox, coyote, wolf

Family: Canidae
Examples: fox, coyote, wolf

Genus: Canis
Examples: coyote, wolf

Species: Canis lupus (wolf)

64

Plants

Unlike animals, plants can't move around; they're fixed to one spot. But they're still alive! Plant life includes everything from little tufts of moss on a tree trunk, through the wide variety of colourful flowers, to giant sequoias – the most massive trees in the world.

Fungi

Fungi look like plants, but they belong to a different group. That's because they don't make their own food like plants do. Instead, they absorb nutrients (substances that living things need to survive) from other materials.

TRUE OR FALSE? The scientific name for the western gorilla is *Gorilla gorilla*. Find out on p.88!

CELLS

Cells are the basic units of life, and all living things have at least one cell. Animals and humans have many more. A blue whale – the largest animal on Earth – has about one hundred quadrillion (that's one hundred thousand trillion) cells in its body.

What do cells do?

In both plants and animals, cells have lots of responsibilities. They contain things that help them obtain energy from food, make chemicals that the body needs, and reproduce to make new cells. Cells also hold everything inside them together, to keep them safe.

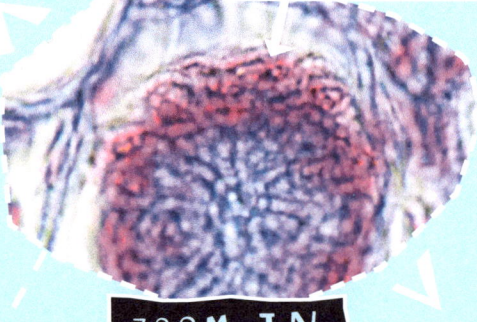

cell membrane

ZOOM IN

The cell membrane keeps everything inside the cell together.

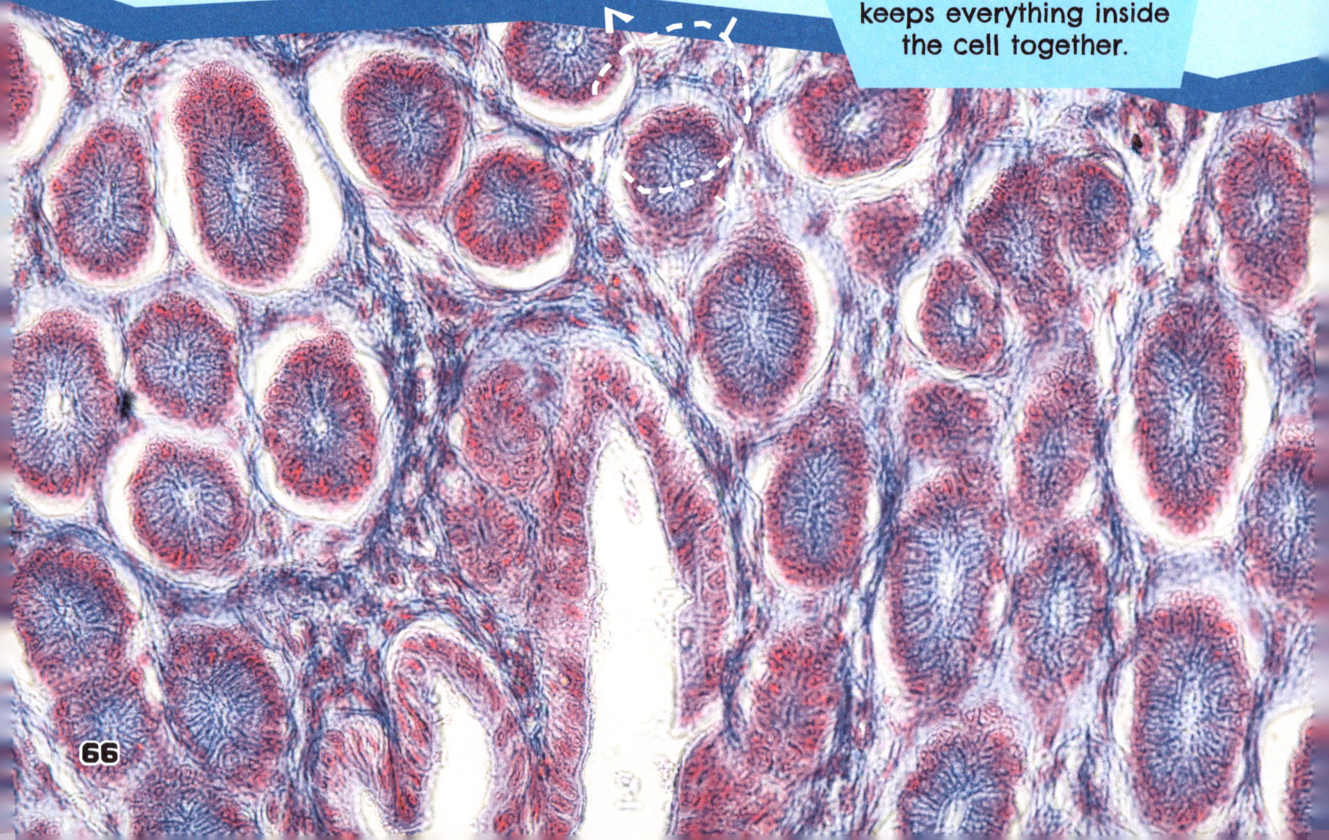

Cell structure

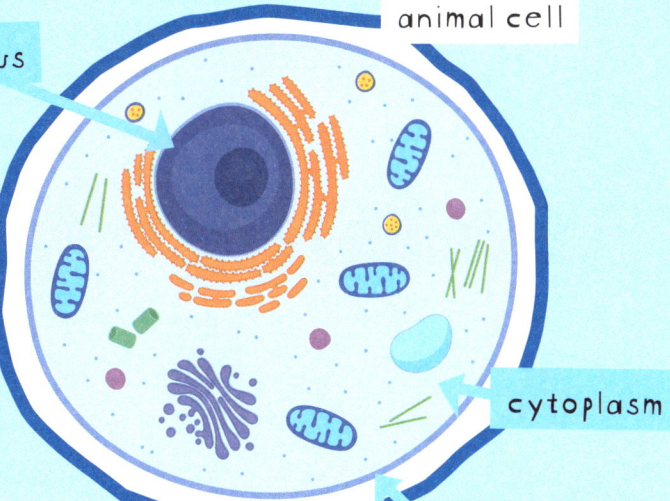

Animal cells have three key parts: nucleus, cytoplasm and cell membrane. The cytoplasm is a jelly-like material. It is where many of the chemical reactions happen in the cell.

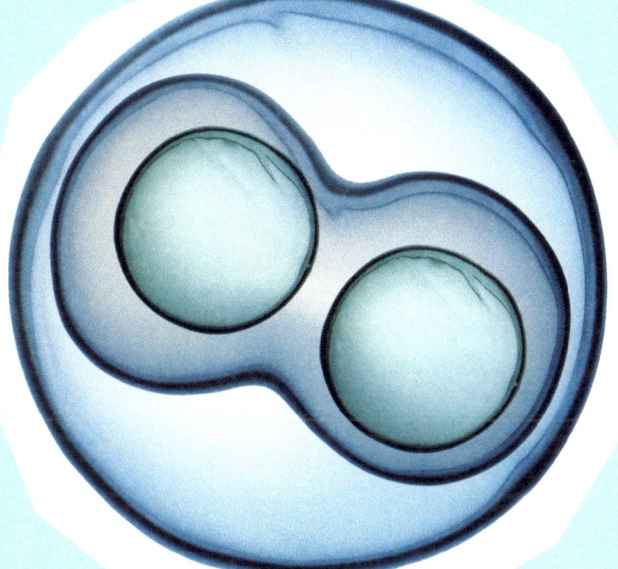

Nucleus

The nucleus is the cell's control centre, keeping everything running smoothly. It's where the cell's genetic material, or DNA, is found (see p.68) and helps to control when the cell divides to make new cells.

How many cells?

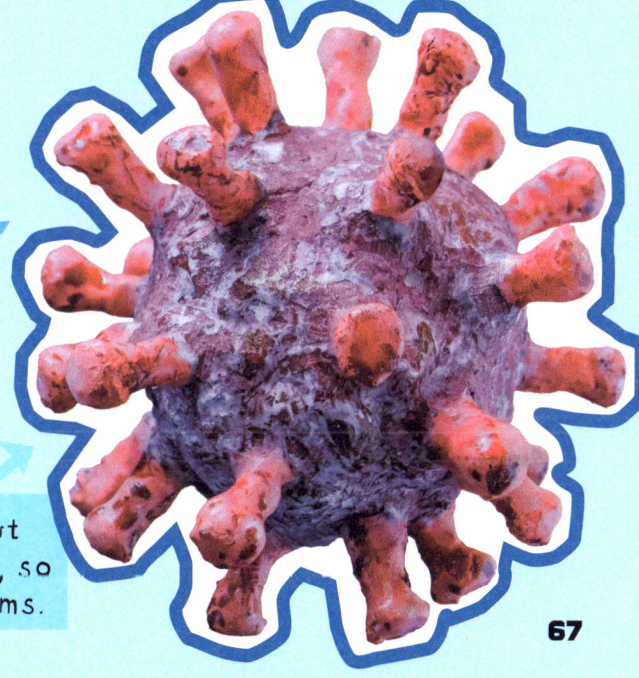

Bacteria and some algae only have one cell. But most organisms grow by cell division to have lots of cells. Whether it's a single-celled bacteria or the trillions of cells in a human body, every cell works to keep itself and the organism alive.

Viruses are a bit like bacteria, but they don't have even a single cell, so they're not seen as living organisms.

DNA

DNA is like an instruction manual for life. It contains all the information that living organisms need to grow and reproduce, whether that's a person, a porcupine or a plant!

It's in your genes

DNA is short for deoxyribonucleic acid. It's tucked inside the nucleus of nearly every cell in every living thing, and it contains a kind of code for how organisms look and function. For example, in animals, DNA determines what colour fur an animal has and how long its tail is. DNA is divided into sections called genes, each of which contains a piece of this information.

The structure of DNA

Each piece of DNA is made up of tiny molecules called nucleotides. These pair up in special ways to form DNA's strange structure – two strands that wind around each other to look like a twisted ladder (known as a double helix). Each rung on the ladder stores genetic information. This is written as a kind of code using combinations of four letters: A, T, G and C.

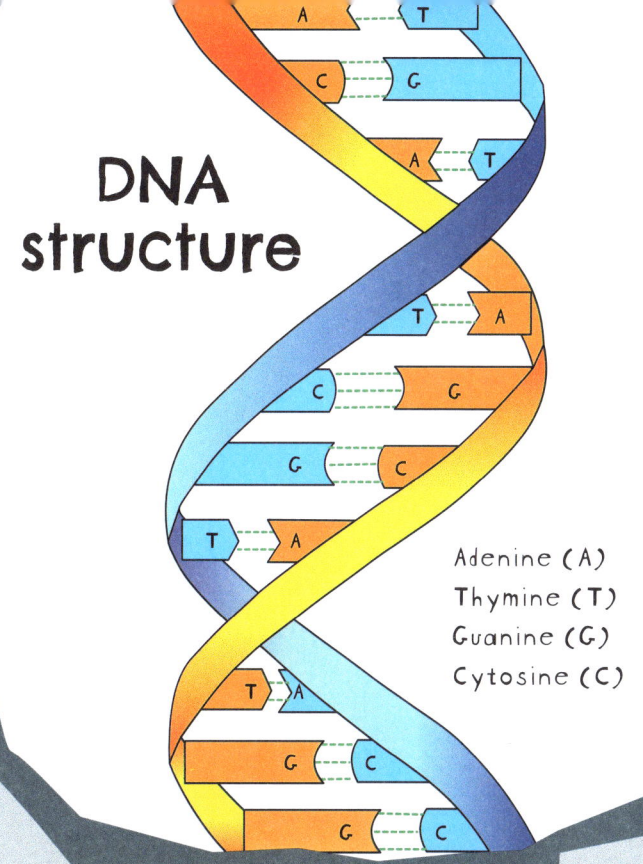

DNA structure

Adenine (A)
Thymine (T)
Guanine (G)
Cytosine (C)

Rosalind Franklin

FAMOUS FIGURE

Scientist Rosalind Franklin (1920–58) used X-rays in an unusual way to learn more about how tiny molecules are arranged. In particular, she looked at the arrangement of molecules in DNA. Her work helped two other scientists, James Watson and Francis Crick, to figure out that DNA had the twisted ladder structure – the double helix.

PLANTS AND PHOTOSYNTHESIS

From plain grass to tall trees, plants are an essential part of the food chain in most habitats on Earth. Without the great variety of plants that grow on land and in water, no animal could survive.

Look, no soil!

All sorts of plants

Most plants grow in soil, drawing up water from their roots. But some plants – for example, algae – live in water. There are even 'air plants', which can grow without soil. They often wind their roots around trees and other plants. There are even some meat-eating plants, which trap insects!

Plants vs. animals

The big difference between plants and animals is how they get their energy. Animals can't make their own food – they get their energy by eating plants or other animals. But plants use an amazing process called photosynthesis to create most of what they need to survive.

ZOOM IN

Stomata are tiny holes on plant leaves and stems that allow plants to take in carbon dioxide and release oxygen.

Photosynthesis

Photosynthesis is a process that uses sunlight, water and carbon dioxide. Plants absorb sunlight through their leaves thanks to a green substance called chlorophyll. At the same time, they take in water from their roots and carbon dioxide from the air. Mixing these together makes a sugar called glucose, which is packed with energy! Plants use glucose as a food, to help them grow.

QUIZ YOURSELF ON...

BIOLOGY

How much have your remembered about biology? Test yourself with these questions...

Check your answers on p.89!

1 How many known species of animal are there?

A. 216,000

B. 2.16 million

C. 216 billion

2 What does the cell membrane do?

A. It holds the cell's DNA.

B. It creates memories.

C. It keeps everything inside the cell together.

3 What is cytoplasm?

A. the jelly-like susbstance inside a cell

B. a type of bacteria

C. a cell's control centre

4 What four letters are used in DNA code?

A. B, A, T and C

B. A, T, G and E

C. A, T, G and C

TRUE OR FALSE? Red blood cells don't contain DNA like other cells do.

Find out on p.88!

5 Which scientist helped James Watson and Francis Crick discover DNA's double helix?

- **A.** Rosalind Franklin
- **B.** Rosalind Helix
- **C.** Rosalind Watson

6 Where does algae live?

- **A.** in the air
- **B.** in water
- **C.** underground

7 What is the big difference between plants and animals?

- **A.** Plants don't have DNA but animals do.
- **B.** Plants can't make their own food but animals can.
- **C.** Animals can't make their own food but plants can.

8 What does photosynthesis produce?

- **A.** new plants
- **B.** glucose
- **C.** bacteria

9 What are stomata?

- **A.** 'stomachs' of plants
- **B.** young tomato plants
- **C.** tiny holes on plant leaves and stems that let them take in oxygen and release carbon dioxide

10 What colour is chlorophyll?

- **A.** green
- **B.** blue
- **C.** black

BUILDINGS AND STRUCTURES

Engineering takes scientific ideas and applies them in the real world. Amazing engineers use science and maths to solve problems and to build things that make life easier, safer and more fun.

Getting to work

Force and motion (see pp.52–53) are important ideas in engineering. Force is the amount of push or pull on an object. Work is the amount of energy it takes to move something over a certain distance. That's where the maths comes in!

$$\text{work done} = \text{force} \times \text{distance}$$

To have enough energy to build big structures like buildings and bridges, you need machines.

Six machines

Using six basic types of machine, engineers can design and build just about anything they want. People have been using these simple machines for thousands of years.

pulley — lever — wheel and axle

wedge — inclined plane — screw

Touching the sky

Skyscrapers are super-tall buildings. Engineers use science to ensure that skyscrapers are safe and sturdy. They study materials, gravity and wind forces to design buildings that won't sway too much in storms, or topple over.

Burj Khalifa

cable-stayed bridge

Bridges

There are lots of different types of bridges, including arch bridges, suspension bridges and cable-stayed bridges. All these designs and materials are tested to make sure they can carry heavy traffic loads and survive extreme weather conditions.

The 5 tallest buildings in the world

1. Burj Khalifa, Dubai, United Arab Emirates (828m)
2. Merdeka 118, Kuala Lumpur, Malaysia (679m)
3. Shanghai Tower, Shanghai, China (632m)
4. Makkah Royal Clock Tower, Makkah, Saudi Arabia (601m)
5. Ping An Finance Center, Shenzhen, China (599m)

VEHICLES

Without science and engineering, how would we get anywhere? Expert engineers put scientific knowledge to good use when designing vehicles.

On the road

Cars are designed to keep us safe and comfortable. Engineers use aerodynamics to create sleek shapes to reduce drag and save on fuel. Strong metals like steel absorb the impact in case of an accident. Airbags and seatbelts use the laws of physics to protect passengers if the car stops suddenly.

In the air

Remember the forces that act on things moving through the air (p.54)? Engineers have to think about these when designing planes. An aeroplane's wings are shaped to create lower air pressure on top and higher pressure below, which 'lifts' the plane.

On the water

Ships float because of buoyancy. Water pushes up on a boat with enough force to stop it from sinking, even when it's huge and carrying a heavy load. The pointed 'nose' and curved back of a boat creates a streamlined shape and helps reduce water resistance.

Riding the rails

Trains use friction to grip the rails, and engineers design train wheels and tracks to reduce resistance and ensure a smooth ride. Some super-streamlined high-speed trains can reach speeds of 320 kilometres per hour.

FASCINATING FACT

Maglev trains use electromagnetism (see p.50) to make them hover above the rails, without touching them at all. Without any friction, they run quickly and smoothly.

COMMUNICATION

We live in a world of instant communication. Technology means we can share information and ideas through talking, text and images in a matter of seconds.

Radio

One of the biggest breakthroughs in communication was the invention of the radio by Italian Guglielmo Marconi in the late nineteenth century. The radio made use of radio waves (see p.43) that could travel through the air to communicate over long distances. In the early 1920s, radio changed from being a communication tool to a source of entertainment and information, and people began to hear news and music in their homes.

Communication developments

1844 The first telegraph message in Morse Code is sent.

1893 Nikola Tesla demonstrates the first practical wireless radio.

1876 Alexander Graham Bell makes the first telephone call.

1937 The first portable two-way radios (walkie-talkies) are used by the military.

The first telephone

Alexander Graham Bell's telephone revolutionised the way people communicated. A microphone turned sound waves into electrical signals, which travelled through wires to another telephone, where it was turned back into sound waves.

Smartphones

Telephones today are very different, of course. Smartphones work like radios, but they're connected to a massive network of towers and satellites. When you call a friend, your voice is turned into digital data, which whizzes through those towers and is decoded into sound at the other end.

1989 The first tablet computer is released – the GRiDPad 1900 – which weighed a whopping 2 kilograms.

2007 The first ever iPhone is released, at a cost of $499 for the 4GB version and $599 for 8GB.

1994 IBM starts selling the first smartphone, called the Simon Personal Communicator.

2009 The WhatsApp instant messaging app is launched.

2020 Zoom announces that 300 million people are attending video meetings every day.

Super Stats

THE INTERNET

The internet officially began in 1983, when different types of computers on different networks were first able to communicate. It took a while to take off, but since then the internet has taken over the world.

Internet users

There are more than 5 billion internet users in the world – that's two-thirds of the global population.

Website numbers

In the middle of 1994, there were just 2,738 websites on the internet. By the middle of 2024 there were more than 1.1 billion, although only about 200 million of them are active.

The speed of information

Internet data travels through fibre-optic cables at nearly the speed of light – that's about 200,000 kilometres per second.

The Internet of Things

By 2030, there may be more than 200 billion devices connected to the internet. Everything from phones to fridges will be joined in a huge 'Internet of Things'.

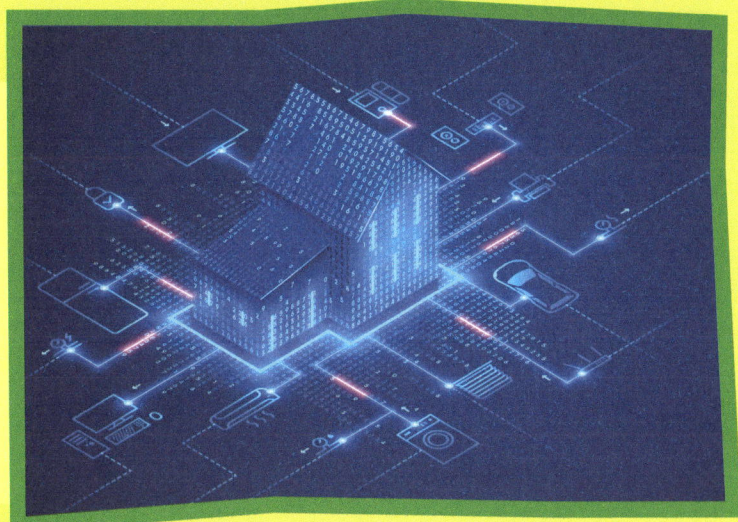

 ## Speedy searching

If you type a search into Google, it normally finds an answer for you in about 0.2 seconds.

 ## Who's Googling?

Google processes about 3.5 billion searches every day – that's about 40,000 every second!

 ## Keeping in touch

More than 350 billion emails are sent every day. On average, people receive 121 emails a day.

 ## Video traffic

More than 80% of all internet traffic is video. Over 500 hours of video are uploaded to YouTube every single minute!

INVENTIONS

For thousands of years, humans have been coming up with inventions to make their lives easier or better. What do you think is the most important invention ever?

Wheel (3500 BC)

It's hard to imagine a time when the wheel didn't exist, but a few thousand years ago even this simple machine would have been considered cutting-edge technology!

Printing press (1440)

Before Johannes Gutenberg's printing press, books had to be copied out by hand. This invention meant that knowledge spread farther and faster than anyone had thought possible.

Batteries (1800)

The electric battery was invented by an Italian physicist called Alessandro Volta. He stacked metal discs with salt water brine or acid in between them, creating the first battery that produced a steady flow of electricity.

Television (1926)

John Logie Baird's mechanical television converted light into electrical impulses – and back again. It changed entertainment technology forever.

Apple Mac (1984)

The first successful personal computer was called the Altair 8800, released in 1974. But it was the first Apple Macintosh in 1984 that revolutionised computers – it was the first mainstream computer with a built-in screen, a mouse and a graphical user interface (GUI).

Wi-Fi (1997)

Wi-Fi launched in 1997, although the name wasn't used for a couple of years. It uses radio waves to transmit data wirelessly, allowing devices to connect to the internet without cables.

FAMOUS FIGURE: Mark E. Dean

Mark E. Dean is a top engineer and computer scientist who has changed the world of printer communication. In the early 1980s, he worked with a colleague to invent a system that helped computers and printers communicate. He now holds 20 patents – licences that prevent others from stealing your ideas – for various inventions.

ROBOTICS

Robotics is a type of engineering where science and technology come together. Robots still sound like something from the future, but they're already operating all around us.

Sensors and sensing

Robots need to understand their surroundings, so they're equipped with cameras and sensors. These are like a robot's eyes and ears, detecting things like light, sound and movement, to stop the robot bumping into things.

Movement and balance

Engineers try to get some robots to move like humans or animals, so they study human movement. For example, by studying human balance and movement, they can build robots that run or climb stairs. By using ideas from physics, engineers have created super-strong robotic arms that can lift heavy objects in factories.

TRUE OR FALSE? Robots can perform surgeries more precisely than human doctors. Find out on p.88!

Special skills

Thanks to artificial intelligence (AI), some robots can learn and even make decisions in a similar way to humans. Robots with AI can improve their abilities over time – for example, self-driving cars learn to read road patterns to drive safely.

I'm here to help!

Robotic arms and legs

One incredible application of robotics is in prosthetics. These are artificial limbs, like arms or legs, that people might have if they lose their own limbs or are born without limbs. Special sensors in the robotic limb are put on the skin over the remaining muscles in a person's own limb. The person can then control the movement of the artificial limb with their thoughts.

Ask an EXPERT about... ENGINEERING

This is Frida Akin-Taylor who trained as a mechanical engineer. She started her engineering career in a role at Rolls-Royce – a multinational aerospace and defence manufacturer.

How did you get into your job?

In year 10, I realised I really loved engineering. I enjoyed learning about different areas of engineering and machining processes, and I always looked forward to engineering classes – they were fun and practical, and they enabled me to apply maths and physics in a way that made sense to me in real life. They also allowed me to manufacture cool things as part of my coursework. I applied for an apprenticeship at Rolls-Royce where they paid for me to go to school and study Mechanical Engineering. While I was learning, I also got to work and gain real-life experience in industry at the same time.

What excites you about your career?

As a manufacturing engineer, my job is to find better ways to make things and to solve problems in factories. When I worked at Rolls-Royce, I helped create ways to safely take apart and put back together the jet engines that power aeroplanes. It was really exciting for me when I saw these huge engines being taken apart and rebuilt because they came from big aeroplanes like the *Boeing 787 Dreamliner*! It felt amazing to see it happen in real life.

What do you do now?

I now work for a global technology company as a senior consultant. I use everything I've learned about engineering to help other companies improve their factories by using new digital tools and technology.

I'm really excited about getting more people interested in STEM (Science, Technology, Engineering, and Maths) subjects. I started a non-profit organisation called Edu-Cater Global, which works in the UK and Kenya. Its goal is to help young people from all backgrounds see how many amazing opportunities STEM can offer them.

How do you think your industry might change in the future?

Within the next few years, I think we'll see the manufacturing industry (the industry that makes lots of things... from clothes to jet engines, and everything in between) relying a lot on digital tools, artificial intelligence (AI) and virtual reality to help produce products much faster and to virtually train workers wherever they are in the world.

ANSWERS

True or false?

p.15: TRUE. A molecule's shape depends on how its electrons and nucleus are arranged.

p.23: TRUE. Mercury is the only liquid metal, although gallium, caesium and rubidium melt very easily at quite low temperatures.

p.29: FALSE. Acids and alkalis cancel each other out, so if the two substances are equally acidic and alkaline, they will combine to make salt and water in a neutralisation reaction.

p.31: TRUE. The raw material for glass is sand, along with limestone and soda ash.

p.36: FALSE. Metals generally conduct electricity very well.

p.49: FALSE. The magnetic force gets weaker the further from the magnet an object is.

p.53: TRUE. Balanced forces cancel each other out, so there is no force to measure.

p.62: FALSE. It's the opposite – smooth surfaces create less friction.

p.65: TRUE. The scientific name for the western lowland gorilla is Gorilla gorilla gorilla!

p.72: TRUE. Red blood cells are very simple cells that carry oxygen around the body, but don't contain DNA.

p.84: TRUE. Surgical robots can perform operations with amazing precision and often assist human doctors when they're doing delicate surgery.

Name that...

pp.18-19: Name that... Chemical element (*possible uses of each element are in italics – although there are many more*)

1. Mercury (Hg) – *thermometers, batteries, dental fillings*
2. Neon (Ne) – *advertising signs*
3. Aluminium (Al) – *aircraft, food packaging, vehicles*
4. Bismuth (Bi) – *medicines, electronics, manufacturing*
5. Gold (Au) – *jewellery*
6. Sodium (Na) – *manufacturing, light bulbs, fire extinguishers*
7. Nickel (Ni) – *stainless steel*
8. Cadmium (Cd) – *batteries, alloys, plastics*
9. Uranium (U) – *nuclear power, medicine, research*
10. Copper (Cu) – *construction, kitchen equipment, tools*
11. Chlorine (Al) – *disinfectant, bleach, manufacturing*
12. Sulphur (S) – *rubber, paper, water treatment*
13. Silver (Ag) – *jewellery, electronics*
14. Lead (Pb) – *cables, shielding systems from x-rays/radiation*

pp.32-33: Name that... Material

1. Rubber
2. Paper
3. Steel
4. Wool
5. Concrete
6. Cotton
7. Diamond
8. Plastic
9. Leather
10. Glass
11. Wood
12. Coal
13. Rock
14. Ceramic

Quiz yourself on...

pp.36-37: Quiz yourself on... Chemistry

1. B. element
2. A. proton
3. B. two
4. C. copper
5. C. graphite
6. A. malleable
7. B. a mixture of two or more metals
8. A. above 7
9. C. wood
10. B. meteorology

pp.62-63: Quiz yourself on... Physics

1. A. kinetic energy
2. C. wind
3. A. visible light
4. C. refraction
5. B. friction
6. C. at both the north and south poles
7. A. The forces cancel each other out.
8. C. newtons
9. B. slows them down
10. C. a force of movement

pp.72-73: Quiz yourself on... Biology

1. B. 2.16 million
2. C. It keeps everything inside the cell together.
3. A. the jelly-like substance inside a cell
4. C. A, T, G and C
5. A. Rosalind Franklin
6. B. in water
7. C. Animals can't make their own food but plants can.
8. B. glucose
9. C. tiny holes on plant leaves and stems that let them take in oxygen and release carbon dioxide
10. A. green

GLOSSARY

air resistance a type of friction that acts on objects moving through the air

alloy a metal created by mixing two or more metal elements e.g. bronze is an alloy of copper and tin

atom tiny particles that are the building blocks of everything on Earth

carbon an element that can form bonds in strong chains with itself and with other elements

cell the basic unit of life – all living things have at least one cell

chemical reaction when two or more elements are put together, they may react with each other to create a new substance

chemistry the study of matter

compound a substance made up of two or more different chemical elements that are chemically combined together

conductor a metal that lets electricity flow through it easily, e.g. copper

DNA short for deoxyribonucleic acid, DNA is the 'code' tucked away inside the nucleus of nearly every cell that controls how organisms look and function

chemical reaction

electrical circuit a closed path or loop that electricity can flow through

electricity a stream of tiny particles called electrons that flow through a metal conductor

electromagnetic spectrum a scale in which different types of light are organised in order of their wavelength

electromagnetism a combination of magnetism and electricity where an electric current is passed through a wire and it creates a magnetic field around it

electron a tiny particle inside an atom that has a negative electrical charge

energy the ability to do work or make things change

force a push or a pull that acts on an object, making it speed up, slow down, change direction or change shape

fossil fuels coal, oil and natural gas – fuels formed from the remains of ancient plants and animals

friction a force that acts to slow objects down

gas when particles in something are spread out so they move freely – gases can expand to fill whatever space they're in

electricity pylons

gravity a force of attraction that pulls things together

insulator a material that doesn't conduct electricity, e.g. plastic – metal electric wires are often coated in plastic to prevent people from getting an electric shock when they touch them

kinetic energy energy of movement

liquid when particles in something are close together, but there's enough room for them to slide around so that a liquid can flow and take the shape of the container it's in

magnetism a force that comes from magnets that pulls magnetic materials towards it

malleable can be bent or shaped without breaking, e.g. the metal, copper, can be bent to create electrical wires

metal a solid material at room temperature (apart from mercury) that can usually be bent or shaped, and is often good at conducting electricity and/or heat

meteorology the scientific study of weather

molecule groups of atoms joined together by chemical bonds called covalent bonds

copper bent into wires

neutron a tiny particle inside an atom that doesn't have an electrical charge

nuclear fission when the nucleus of an atom is split, releasing a huge amount of energy in the form of heat and light

ore metals that are combined with other elements in the ground, e.g. iron ore

periodic table a table that charts all of the discovered chemical elements

photosynthesis the process that plants carry out to produce energy to help them grow – sunlight + water + carbon dioxide = glucose (energy)

physics the study of how the world works and how objects, forces and energy interact

plasma when natural gas gets so hot that some of its electrons break free from their atoms or molecules – it's found in things like stars and lightning

proton a tiny particle inside an atom that has a positive electrical charge

reflection when light can't pass through an object, it usually reflects off it, but back to front

refraction when light passes from one material to another, it bends – or refracts – because light travels at different speeds through different materials

renewable resources energy sources that will never run out, e.g. solar and wind power

solid when particles in something are packed closely together so that a solid can keep its shape and volume

technology the result of applying science to make things that can perform tasks or solve problems

water resistance a type of friction that acts on objects moving through the water

weather a constantly changing system where the Sun, air and water all interact

harnessing wind power

lightning strikes during a storm

INDEX

acceleration 58–60
acid 28, 29, 82
aerodynamics 76
AI (artificial intelligence) 85–87
air pressure 34, 76
air resistance 54, 55, 59
Albert Einstein 57
Alessandro Volta 82
Alexander Graham Bell 79
algae 67
alkali 28, 29
alkali metal 17, 23
alloy 22
Apple Mac 83
astronomy 9
atmosphere 34, 35
atom 11–15, 20, 21, 26, 27, 41
atomic number 16, 17
bacteria 67
battery 46, 82
Bell, Alexander Graham 79
biology 9, 64–71
bond 14, 15, 20, 26, 27
buckyballs 21
building 74, 75
buoyancy 77
car 76
carbon 20, 21, 27, 30
cell 66–68

cell membrane 66, 67
chain (food) 70
charge 12, 35, 47
chemical element 12, 18, 19
chemical reaction 8, 26, 27, 67
chemistry 8, 10–35
chlorophyll 71
coal 40
colour 42, 43
communication 78–81, 87
compass 51
compound 15
computer 39, 79–81, 83
conductor 23, 46
covalent bond 14, 15
Crick, Francis 69
cytoplasm 67
Dean, Mark E. 83
diamond 20
DNA 67–69
double helix 69
drag 59, 61, 76
Edison, Thomas 47
Einstein, Albert 57
electrical circuit 46
electrical energy 39
electricity 8, 23, 27, 35, 40, 41, 46, 47, 50, 82
electromagnetic spectrum 43

electromagnetism 50, 51, 77
electron 11–15, 46, 47
element 14–27
emergency stop 61
energy 13, 27, 38–41, 71, 74
engineering 74–77, 83–87
equation 27
Ernest Rutherford 13
food chain 70
force 52–55, 58–61, 74
fossil fuel 40
Francis Crick 69
Franklin, Rosalind 69
friction 47, 54, 55, 61, 77
fuel 38, 40, 76
fungi 65
gas 11, 40
gear 59
gene 67–69
genetic material 67
glucose 71
gravitational pull 56
gravity 53, 56, 57, 60, 75
Guglielmo Marconi 78
Gutenberg, Johannes 82
heat 13, 21, 27, 34, 39, 41, 55
helix (double) 69
hydroelectricity 41
ice 10, 11, 54

94

inclined plane 74
insulator 46, 47
internet 39, 80, 81, 83
invention 82, 83
ion 14, 15
Isaac Newton 53
James Watson 69
Johannes Gutenberg 82
John Logie Baird 83
kinetic energy 39
lever 59, 74
life 64–71
light 39, 42, 43
light bulb 46, 47
lightning 11, 35, 42
liquid 10
Logie Baird, John 83
machine 59, 74
Maglev 77
magnetism 48–51, 60, 61
malleable 22
Marconi, Guglielmo 78
Mark E. Dean 83
mass 57
material 30–33
matter 10–13
metal 22–25, 76, 82
meteorology 34, 35
microphone 79
molecule 11, 14, 15, 21, 69
Moon 44, 60
motion 58, 59, 74
movement 84, 85
MRI machine 50
network 80, 81
neutron 12, 13
Newton, Isaac 53
newtons 53
nodding donkey 40
nuclear energy 13
nuclear fission 13

nuclear power 41
nucleotide 69
nucleus (atom) 12, 13
nucleus (cell) 67, 68
oil 40
ore 23
particle 10, 11, 14, 15, 35, 46
periodic table 16, 17
pH scale 29
photosynthesis 70, 71
physics 8, 38–61, 76, 77, 84, 85
plant 65, 70, 71
plasma 11
plastic 30, 31, 46
potential energy 39
power station 47
printing press 82
prism 43
prosthetic 85
proton 12, 13
pulley 59, 74
radio 78
radio wave 78
rainbow 43
reflection 44, 45
refraction 44, 45
renewable resource 41
resistance 54, 55, 59, 61, 77
robotics 84, 85
rock 10, 30, 31
Rosalind Franklin 69
Rutherford, Ernest 13
satellite 79
screw 74
shadow 42
ship 77
skyscraper 75
smartphone 39, 79, 86
solar power 41
solar wind 51

solid 10
sound wave 79
space 8, 20, 21, 55, 56, 57, 60
speed 58, 59, 61
stars 11, 21
state 10, 11
static electricity 47
stomata 71
subatomic particle 12
sunlight 27, 38, 41–43, 71
supernova explosion 21
technology 9, 78–87
telephone 78, 79
television 83
Thomas Edison 47
thrust 59
thunder 35
tidal power 41
train 77
transport 38
turbine 41
vehicle 76, 77
virtual reality (VR) 87
virus 67
Volta, Alessandro 82
water resistance 55, 61, 77
water vapour 35
Watson, James 69
wave (radio) 78
wave (sound) 79
wavelength 43
weather 34, 35
website 80, 81
wedge 74
weight 57
wheel 82
wheel and axle 74
Wi-Fi 83
wind power 41
work done 74
X-ray 69

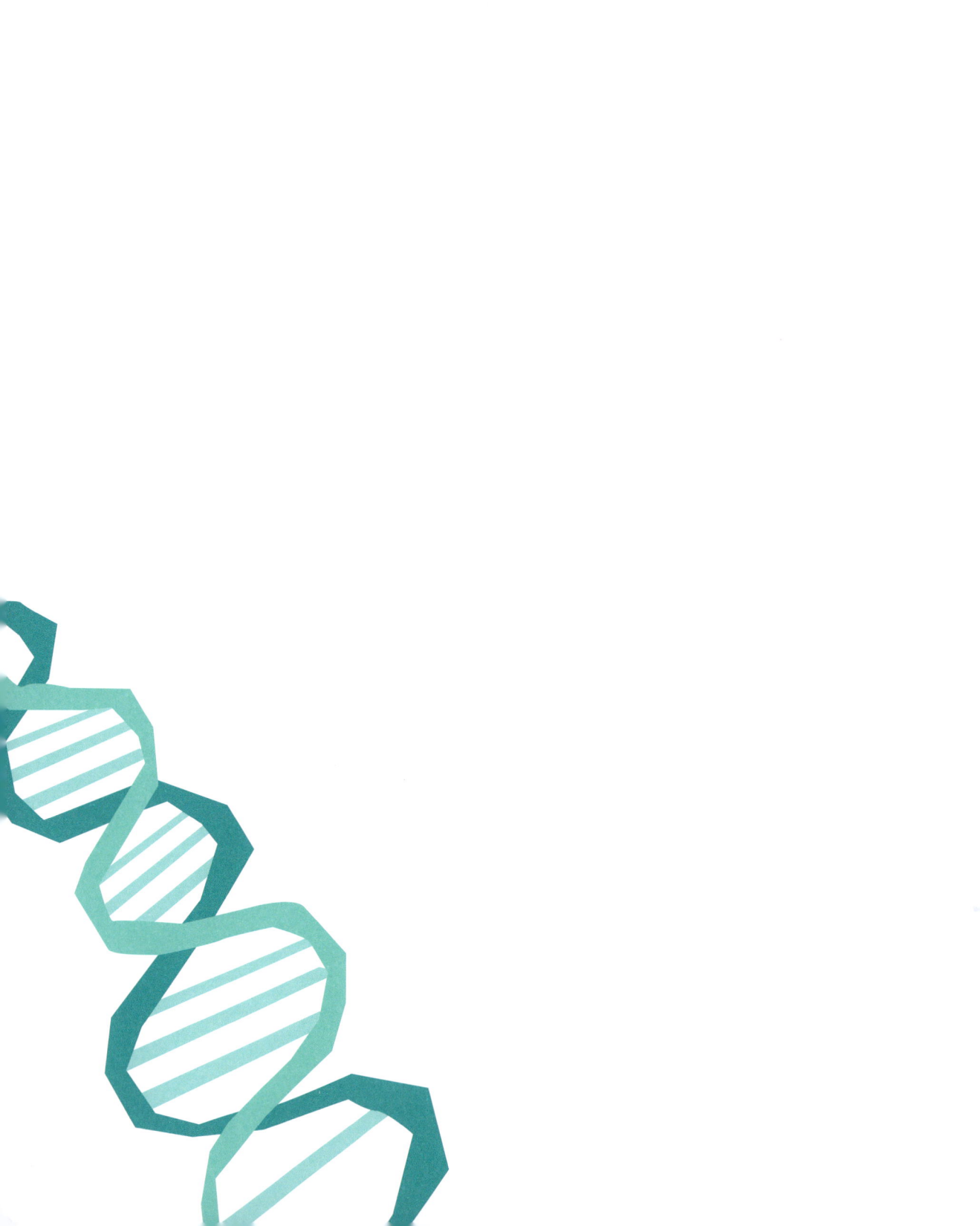